HARRY ARMFIELD

COOL

THE COMPLETE HANDBOOK

Druce
Please read with
great care — I mean it
you don't get it together now
will you ever !!!
Love
Alan

PAVILION
MICHAEL JOSEPH

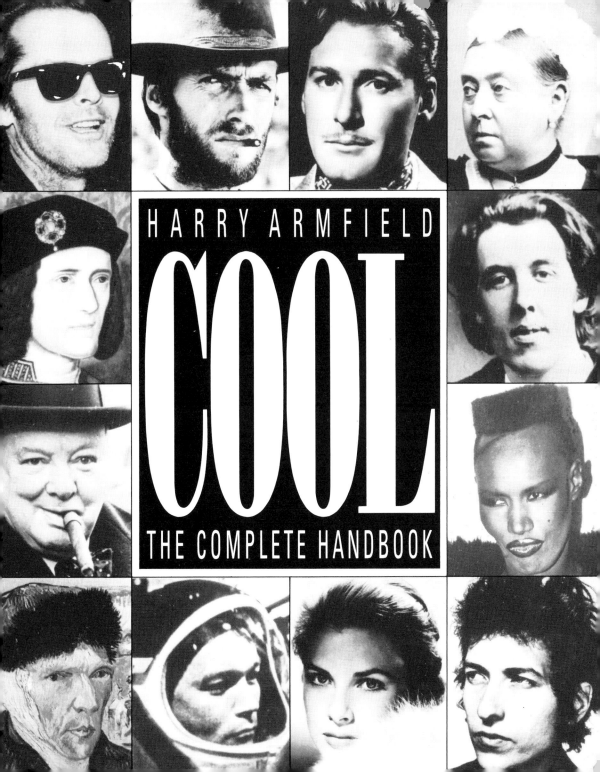

HARRY ARMFIELD

COOL

THE COMPLETE HANDBOOK

DEDICATED TO

The Cool Couple
at Coombe Cottage

First published in Great Britain in 1986 by
Pavilion Books Limited
196 Shaftesbury Avenue, London WC2H 8JL
in association with Michael Joseph Limited
27 Wrights Lane, Kensington, London W8 5TZ

Armfield, Harry
The complete cool handbook
1. Manners and customs
I. Title
302 GT76
ISBN 1-85145-088-2

Typeset by Dorchester Typesetting,
Dorchester
Printed and bound in Great Britain by
Butler and Tanner Limited, Frome, Somerset

Contents

A Question of I.D.   6

What Makes the Cool Spirit?   8

Rules   10

A Brief History   14

Races and Tribes   20

The Cool Code
    the Enigma and its Variations   24

Growing Up with It   34

Breeding Grounds   36

Making a Career of It   38

Living   42

Drink   48

Sustenance   51

Mean Streets   53

Couples   60

Dinner Parties   63

Music   67

Dying to be Cool   76

Body Heat   78

Fashion   85

Accessories After the Fact   94

Medium Cool   99

Sports and Pastimes   132

Conclusions   138

ARE YOU? Have you ever been? Are you ever likely to be? Cool. Will you ever attain that elevated status, that rarefied condition which separates mere mortals from the gods, the wheat from the chaff, the men from the boys?

Are you a King Kong or a King Dong? A dude or a dud? A desperado or just plain desperate?

Look in the mirror. Do you tremble at what stands before you, or can't you see for the cracks? Do others wear sunglasses in your presence, or is it simply the clothes you wear?

What's cool in the Eighties? Can it be measured in negative degrees Celsius? And what role, if any, does it play in a post-war nuclear suburban class-conscious society?

Has Michael Fish got any? Will Johnnie Ordinary acquire any when he swaps his Cortina for a Corvette?

If you don't have the answers then it's time you did. Cool is the word on everyone's lips. If you're not cool, you're nowhere. Without cool, people will treat you like a doormat, laugh like hyenas at your physical shortcomings, and steal the last mouthful of filet mignon from your plate.

It's time to learn the hidden truth about the Big Chill.

It's time to call it in.

But first a test –

A Question of I.D.

THE FIRST TEST

PART ONE

Answer Yes or No.

1. Can you strike a match with the edge of your thumb-nail without setting fire to your hand?

2. Can you tell the difference between Kelly le Brock and Kelly Emberg in the dark?

3. Do people sift through the rubbish in your dustbins for clues to your spiritual and biogenetic make-up?

4. Do mothers drag their children off the streets when you ride into town?

5. Have you ever given yourself a blood transfusion?

6. Do people collect your broken fingernails before you've had a chance to swallow them?

7. Has anyone ever performed ritual suicide outside your home because you rejected them?

8. Have you ever appeared in a Martini or a Maxell TV commercial?

9. Have you ever appeared in a Milton Keynes commercial? (Trick question.)

10. Can you play the complete chord sequence of 'Sultans of Swing'?

PART TWO

Multiple choice.

1. Which scores higher?
   a) Street cred.
   b) Radical chic.
   c) Cult status.
   d) Not giving a monkey's.

2. Which would you wear to a Tatler fancy dress bash?
   a) Yves St Laurent.
   b) Ysatis.
   c) Eve Marie Saint.
   d) None of these since Mark Boxer didn't invite you.

3 From the following names, can you discover the secret of directing a French film?
a) Jean Luc Besson.
b) Jean Luc Godard.
c) Jean Jacques Beineix.
d) Jean Cocteau.
e) Jean Renoir.
f) Jean Vigo.

4 Which event was cooler?
a) The Beatles playing on top of the Apple building.
b) Neil Armstrong setting the first foot on the moon.
c) The discovery of the tremolo arm.
d) Hannibal crossing the Alps.
e) Claire Francis circumnavigating the world single-handedly.

5 Which blood group is more expensive?
a) B.
b) A.
c) O+.
d) AB−.
e) Keith Richard's.

7

What Makes the Cool Spirit?

Cool is dictionary-defined as not being affected by passion or emotion; unexcited; deliberate; calm; deficient in ardour, interest or zeal; wanting in cordiality (the desire for a 7-Up?); calmly audacious or impudent in making a proposal or demand.

The dictionary is a good starting point and it certainly helps fill up a lot of valuable writing space, but what can we learn from the good book?

Basically, if it's individual, it's good. The spirit of the individual is everything. It's what you are. It's your personality. It's all about you. It doesn't necessarily come overnight and there are many lessons you can learn. You can also cheat – i.e. take aspects of someone else's individuality and mould it to your own. But don't confuse cool with chic or style. Cool is not interested in male models, mannequins, matinee idols, or so-called arbiters of style. Cool is just cool. Nothing else.

There are only two people who count. Mr. and Miz Cool –

MR. AND MIZ COOL

Mr. and Miz Cool are essentially single (see *cool couples* for the exceptions). For them individuality is everything, self-sufficiency is all. The Cools have many friends, many admirers, many lovers, though these are changed with the regularity of their Calvin Klein underwear. When lovers are shed, they don't go haywire and blow up a busload of innocent pensioners on a day's outing, rather they're too awed by their rare experience and suicide is usually the last thing on their minds. To have a suicide dumped on your doorstep is literally the end of the line for both of you.

Mel and Sigourney as Mr and Miz Cool in The Year of Living Dangerously.

C O O L

RULE ONE

THE UNLIKELIEST
PEOPLE ARE COOL

ONE thing should be quite clear from the start. Cool is not all black leather, dark shades, indecipherable grunts and crinkly smiles. Sexual attraction has its place, as does carefully coiffeured but strategically roughed up hair, but let's not forget NHS spex, bent noses and awkward lumps.

It has been known for fat to be cool, baldness to shine, and absolute extreme cases of ugliness . . . well they have also elicited the odd stunned silence.

THE FAT, THE BALD
AND THE UGLY

Truman Capote
When alive, not tall or handsome in the slightest (ie short and hideous), but it didn't stop him becoming a darling of the New York glitterati.

Orson Welles
'F' for Fat, but also 'F' for Fake and Fab masterpiece *Citizen Kane*.

Charles Laughton
He out-Quasied Quasimodo but his one and only directorial effort, *Night of the Hunter*, was a masterly piece of film direction.

Marlon Brando
The uglier and balder he gets, the bigger his movie fee. Reputed to have been paid $2 million for an appearance lasting a handful of minutes in *Superman*. To say nothing of his percentage of the profits.

Henry Kissinger
Living proof that power is princely even if you look like a toad.

OF MICE AND MEN,
COWARDS AND WIMPS

No need to be a machoid of the species or a muscle-bound lamebrain when you can get away with being a spineless, gutless heel and survive through an abundance of charm and immaculate self-effacing wit.

Bob Hope
He made a career out of a suave approach to cowardice. Despite persistent intimidation, he always retained both his credibility *and* the girl by the end of every film.

Woody Allen

The archetypal wimp, sand in the face is too good for him. He could have modelled for x-ray spex but instead developed an original brand of intelligent comedy that charmed the pants off Keaton, Rampling and Farrow in quick succession.

And let's not forget all those scenes when 'the coward' finally breaks. An innocent puppy has been mal-treated. The bad guys leer and scorn. You can hear the Jaws music stir as our hero moves into action, and my God, he's not even wearing a gun.

Buster Keaton, George Best, Steve Martin's *Jerk* and *Eraserhead* to name but a few. Cool failures repre-sent all those who lose the heroine to the handsome stereotype, but redeem themselves by holding the enemy hordes at bay with nothing but a stick of dynamite and a half-chewed cigar stub.

SERVANTS

Servants as puppet masters, mas-ters as puppets. Dirk Bogarde in *The Servant*. Oddjob in *Goldfinger* and Genet's *The Maids*. Many are found in Shakespeare's plays, e.g. Iago in *Othello*, Enobarbus in *Anthony and Cleopatra*. They some-times come in the form of butlers, Jeeves being the most famous, and *The Admirable Crichton*, who turned the tables on his aristocratic masters when they were marooned on a desert island after a ship-wreck.

THE INSANE

The insane cool generally act like Anthony Perkins playing Donald Pleasance or vice versa. Those de-serving to win an Oscar for the best OTT performance: James Cagney in *White Heat*, Rutger Hauer in *Blade Runner* and *The Hitcher*, and all of those actors who played Scarface at one time or another.

WEIRDOES, ECCENTRICS AND RECLUSES

These all have their examples, even if they're only discovered by proxy, or through unauthorized biog-raphies and asylum windows.

Howard Hughes

Former film director, playboy, de-signer of cantilevered brassieres, test pilot and aircraft designer. Hughes was a fallen angel of cool since he ended up spending his countless millions on Kleenex and bog paper.

Paul Getty

Once the world's richest man and a latterday recluse, he charged in-terest on his grandson's ransom payment.

Van Gogh
The brilliant but commercially un-
successful artist who dismantled
half his left-sided hearing capacity
because he couldn't paint it right.

Spike Milligan
Every generation's favourite luna-
tic.

NOT FORGETTING . . .

The animal kingdom Lassie. Rin-
Tin-Tin, Walt Disney's Perri the
squirrel.

**And a whole host of animated
characters** Shultz's beagle Snoopy.
Hergé's Tintin and Snowy. Topcat
and his gang of felonious felines.

ERNEST HEMINGWAY
"THE RICH ARE DIFFERENT
FROM US"

F. SCOTT FITZGERALD
"YES, THEY HAVE MORE
MONEY"

R U L E T W O
MONEY ISN'T
EVERYTHING

Being loaded doesn't automatically
make you cool, although having a
certain amount of the folding stuff
gives you a head start.

The point is, you've got to
know how to use whatever cash you
have properly. Spend it on the
wrong things, spend it on bad taste
and grandiose follies and you'd be
better off being a character out of a
Zola novel.

Without the readies, looks
and street sass certainly take on a
more demanding role. Your cool
really has to work for you.

With limited funds you have
to box clever. Some decent threads
and an ability to communicate will
help to put you on the right track.

Cool needn't be expensive but
it can cost.

Some people have been
known to achieve questionable cool
by giving their money away. The
ex-lead guitarist of Fleetwood Mac,
Peter Green, gave away all his cash
and became a grave digger.
(See also *Dole Cool*.)

R U L E   T H R E E
NO MORE HEROES

The cool rarely have heroes or heroines. They themselves are the heroes and heroines of the piece. Rare exceptions to the 'no heroes rule' will be obscure artists, thinkers, humanitarians and plain 'ornery folk who are salt of the earth material, eg Lou Grant, Sher-

pa Tensing, Dame Freya Stark, Manny Shinwell, Vladimir Horowitz, etc.

Beware of anyone who refers to Bruce Springsteen as 'the Boss'.

R U L E   F O U R
NO VOLVOS

If you have to ask why, go to the back of the class.

The only possible exception to this rule is the P1800 Sports model popularized by *The Saint* TV series.

If you really have to ask why 'no Volvos', read my seminal work on the subject, *Volvos for Dildos*.

R U L E   F I V E
NO RULES

Naturally cool people don't play anything by the rules, except perhaps cricket. Rules were made to be broken OK, so forget everything that's gone before (except the one about Volvos).

COOL wasn't invented overnight along with Jimmy Dean, pop music and the movies. Cool transcends history. The good that men do lives on after them and all that jazz. Death itself doesn't alter cool, it simply brings the sum total of its parts into focus and presents the result to a captive audience.

Whether cool was a moment, an event or someone's life in total, it will be remembered. Even if it's in the moment of their death – the way in which they died, despite an unspectacular life – that can be the coolest moment of all. (See *Dying To Be Cool*.)

Obituaries will usually make the subject seem larger than life since they condense a lifetime's efforts into a few lines of prose. (No one ever mentioned the later life of Sir Francis Drake, by all accounts a failure, or what Katie did next.) But perhaps that's as it should be.

WHO INVENTED IT?

God? Certainly if he hadn't started the whole business, the Rayban factory would have gone out of business long ago.

Adam and Eve? They blew it instantly. One forbidden apple and the Garden of Eden is off limits forever. Trespassers will be blown away and everyone gets to inherit 'Original Sin'.

A Cool Brief History

Cain gets some credit for topping his wimpy brother **Abel**.

Noah built the ark while the rest of the neighbourhood jeered. They obviously forgot to check out the weather forecast for the next six months.

Moses He parted the Red Sea in the same way the Fonz gets a juke-box to work.

And little fourth division **David** beat top-of-the-table first division **Goliath** one-nil at home to win the Philistine Associates Cup fifth round replay.

Buddha (*c.* 563-483 BC) 'The Enlightened.' A rajah's son distressed by the problem of human suffering he gave himself up to the religious life. His teaching is summarized in the 'four noble truths' and the 'eightfold path'. He's still very popular and does a nice line in cute little statues.

Confucius (551-479 BC) The hip Chinese philosopher preaches reason, love, forgiveness and respect for his fellow man. Later, for no apparent reason, he would lengthen his name to Confucius-He-Says.

Alexander the Great (356-323 BC) Educated by Aristotle. Legend has it that he conquered the whole of the civilized world by age twenty-six (something not even *Dynasty* has managed). Died young. Stayed pretty.

Spartacus (*c.* 108-71 BC) Thracian rebel. A slave and gladiator, Spart escaped captivity and headed an insurrection. He routed several Roman armies before being captured on film by Stanley Kubrick and summarily executed for overacting. In fact, he was simply replaced by Kirk Douglas.

Cleopatra (*c.* 69-30 BC) Lover of Caesar and Mark Anthony. Her barge journey up the Nile en route to her first date with Julius and her rolling-out-of-a-carpet act had them turning over in the pyramids.

John the Baptist (early AD) J.C.'s buddy. He wasn't going to be sexually blackmailed by Salome even though he paid a high price for his decision.

J.C. (early AD 1-33) Amongst his miracles he fed the five thousand with five loaves and a couple of fish and provided alcoholic refreshments after hours when he turned water into wine. He always turned a cheek when he could've annihilated the opposition both physically and verbally.

King Arthur (*c.* AD 600) Along with creating the mystique of Camelot and capturing the beautiful Guinevere, he invented the round table so all his knights could feel equal. Lancelot, unfortunately, felt more equal than everyone else and seduced Guinevere without permission. No one seems to have held this instance of cockoldry against King Art, and his cool remains intact.

The Black Prince (1330-1376) No one knows much about the Black Prince except that he had a great name, a black horse and won a great victory at Crécy.

Richard III (1452-1485) Did he really kill the little princes? Probably not. But who cares if he did? Richard turned evil into an art form, which has since been much copied,

but never so stylishly. Great posture. Great last words 'A horse. A horse. My Kingdom for a horse.'

Leonardo da Vinci (1452-1519) Painter, architect, philosopher, poet, sculptor, athlete, mathematician, inventor, anatomist and ace writer. An all-round genius who recorded his scientific work in unfinished notebooks written from right to left, so they would only be understood by people who owned mirrors. Truth is often stranger than fiction.

Niccolo Machiavelli (1469-1527) A good century for Italians. Mac was a Florentine renaissance diplomat and theorist of the modern state. His book *The Prince* remains a seminal study for the power-mad.

Giovanni Casanova (1725-1798) Mainly remembered for having had a thoroughly good time with an exceptionally large number of women.

Horatio Nelson (1758-1805) Forever surrounded by the thunder of battle even when at home with his mistress Emma Hamilton. Nelson's brilliant sea record ended with his death at Trafalgar. Mystery still surrounds the exactness of his final words ('Kiss me Hardy'? 'Kismet Hardy'? 'Kiss me? Hardly!').

Duke of Wellington (1769-1852) Defeated Napoleon at Waterloo. Great boots. Great quote, '*Publish and be damned*', spoken to his mistress when she revealed she was going to blow the whistle on their affair.

Benjamin Disraeli (1804-1881) Jewish, dandy, novelist. John Bright summed him up perfectly when he said, '*He is a self-made man and worships his creator*'. Befriended Queen Victoria through his charm – 'We authors, ma'am . . .' Bought the Suez Canal.

Lord Byron (1788-1824) Poet, romantic, faggy dresser and expert seducer. Nevertheless the author of the excellently titled *Hours of Idleness* (see **Dole Cool**) which was violently attacked by the Edinburgh Review.

Queen Victoria (1819-1901) For her role in introducing water closets into society and for her Royal 'We': ('We are not amused').

Sitting Bull (1831-1890) Indian chief who wiped the smile off the face of the American establishment, and more than the smile off the face of Custer when he won the Battle of the Little Big Horn.

Alfred Nobel (1833-1896) Discovered dynamite. Amassed a fortune. Founded the peace prizes and made possible many a Clint Eastwood/Lee Van Cleef movie.

Oscar Wilde (1854-1900) Into boys and literary excellence, he gets a section to himself (see **The Oscars**).

Sir Winston Churchill (1874-1965) His 'We shall fight them on the beaches' speech got 'em going in 1940, as did his throat-slitting replies to personal detractors.

Mata Hari (1876-1917) The most notorious spy since Delilah and the most accomplished mistress since

La Pompadour. She had everyone on both sides, literally.

Pablo Picasso (1881-1973) Like Rubik, Pic was a Cubist as well as being a major influence in contemporary art. When he was famous and rich enough not to need the money, he used to pay his restaurant bills with a quick tablecloth sketch.

Lawrence of Arabia (1888-1935) For the legend, if not the truth of his flamboyant leadership of the Arabs *v*. Turks during WW1. Great outfits and exploits, blowing up trains, riding round on camels, etc. He wrote a very boring book, only redeemed by its great title – *The Seven Pillars of Wisdom*.

John F. Kennedy (1917-1963) Charismatic US President who, amongst other things, was befriended by Marilyn Monroe.

Bob Geldof, KBE (b. 1952) For his 'Fuck-the-address-and-send-us-the-money' activities. And for his 'You're a bunch of thugs' speech to the United Nations.

And last but not least, the German Luftwaffe ace who, with the tide of the Battle of Britain going against him, was asked by Goering what could be done to help. He replied: *'I'd like a squadron of Spitfires.'*

THOSE WHO DIDN'T MAKE IT

Henry V (1050-1106) Outstanding monarch and general but had little English meadow-cred because of his pudding bowl haircut.

Robin Hood (*circa* 12C) An original idea: to rob the rich and give to the poor (ie himself). But he ruined it by both lousy tailoring (tights, *green* suede shoes) and being far too merry to be cool.

George Armstrong Custer (1839-1876) Far too vain and effeminate. A spiky comeuppance winged its way to him at the Little Big Horn.

Sir Walter Raleigh (1552-1618) Did he really lay his brand new threads over a muddy puddle so a queen could step on it? It's known they do that kind of thing at the Heaven nightclub in London – but in medieval England?

Benito Mussolini (1883-1945) A distant relative of Colonel Gaddafi. Few people had his energy to act the fool twenty-four hours a day, even if he did make the trains run on time. He even once managed to miss an assassin's bullet because his chin was tilted up so high.

Joan of Arc (1412-1431) Such a little goody-goody, burning was too good for her.

Tsar Nick (1868-1918) You can't keep a good revolution down. He gave us *Dr. Zhivago* and Julie Christie, but for him and his family it was the great archipelago in the sky.

Count Dracula (throughout time). The biggest ham since Pinky and Perky.

Yasser Arafat (b. 1929) He failed his audition for ZZ Top and takes it out on the rest of the civilized world.

Yasser Arafat. Failing his audition for ZZ Top

Heinrich Himmler (1900-1945) Unimaginative mass murderer. His last words were 'I am Heinrich Himmler'.

Teddy Kennedy (b. 1932) U.S. senator, brother of Bobby and JFK. He drives a lady friend into a lake but forgets to save her life and thereby destroys his political career.

Gerald Ford (b. 1913) Anyone whose reputation is summed up by the following epithets doesn't have a hope in hell –
'He played too much football without a helmet.'
'He can't eat gum and walk at the same time.'
'He'd fuck up a two-car funeral.'

Gerald Ford. Trying to play tennis and talk on the phone simultaneously

Rudolf Hess (b. 1894) Buddy of Adolf's. Having helped start WW2. he flies to Scotland to negotiate peace. To his surprise they lock him up and throw away the key.

Alfred the Great (AD 849-899) A fine reputation flushed straight down the pan because the idiot goes and burns the cakes. Unable to salvage his reputation, his PRO goes bankrupt and Alf never recovers.

Races and Tribes

IF YOU have trouble shining on your own, it's still possible to shine in a corporate kind of way as member of a subway sect, a heavy brigade, a warrior tribe or as part of an old civilization. In recent times, the emphasis is placed more on the individual, since the cult of the lone-wolf seems to be where it's at in the Eighties. Nevertheless, there's still Greenpeace, Live Aid, VSO and the Peace Corps to consider. Not to mention the corporate spirit of the Olympic Games, the fraternity of rock climbers and the aesthetic athleticism of the Corps de Ballet.

The Ancient Chinese A civilization that lasted four thousand years and gave us paper, gunpowder, the compass and civilized government, while the rest of us were still busy crawling around in the swamps.

The Vikings (8th-11th C) Join the Vikings and see the world. Piracy on the high seas. Raping and pillaging with a bunch of your closest mates and accidentally discovering America five hundred years before Columbus. Magic.

The Incas (c. 1100-1530) Worshipped the sun, lived in peace and kept no weapons. Despite violent destruction at the hands of the Spanish conquistadors they approached death with stoicism and dignity.

The Druids (Ages ago) Magicians posing as priests in ancient times. Strange comings and goings, weird signs and prophecies. Stonehenge. The Avebury Rings. Ley lines. The future meets the past.

The Red Indians (pre-white man) With all that huntin', shootin', fishin', ridin', scalpin' and a-squawin', Red Indians had more going for them than the whole of Club Med put together. This wonderfully cool existence was later replaced with a more sober one named America.

The Cult of the Black Virgin Great name. Who cares what they do as long as they send you a membership card that'll get you into Tramp or Annabel's, no questions asked.

U.N.C.L.E. Despite reaching its heyday in the Sixties, U.N.C.L.E. is still going strong today, fighting against the international discom-

COOL

fort of THRUSH. Remember, wherever you are, whatever you're doing, you may be called on to drop everything and fly to Istanbul where you will be contacted by a club-footed man in a Dylan Thomas suit.

The Samurai (11th-19th C) The military caste in feudal Japan that fervently believed in the concept of death with honour. Great outfit. Great sword. The spirit lives on in consumer driven Japan, in the memory of Yukio Mishima who publicly disembowelled himself for the cause *(see Dying To Be Cool).*

UNCOOL RACES AND TRIBES

The National Front A type of Neo-Nazism continuing themes similar to those laid down by the Führer, ie racial purity, world domination and sundry other old chestnuts. Uber alles cool people are never extremists.

Soccerus Hooliganus They left their marbles behind on the terraces in the Sixties and unfortunately never got them back. For some inexplicable reason the Soccerus Hooliganus confuses a jolly little ball game with ultra violent acts of mayhem.

Iranian Students This species hung out in the Union bars of the Seventies and spent their foreign grants playing bar-football. Having nearly overrun the world during that period, they seem less of a threat nowadays.

Luxembourg Citizen Where are you? What do you look like? Can anyone name a famous Luxembourger?

Hell's Angels Now mainly used by Hollywood as a form of light relief in the movies. The hapless hero runs into a bunch of Angels, escapes after neatly knocking their bikes down like dominoes. They catch up with him only to be beaten to a pulp by his girlfriend.

The Swiss *'Remember what the man said ... "In Italy for thirty years under the Borgias they had warfare, terror, murder, bloodshed, but they produced Michelangelo, Leonardo da Vinci, and the Renaissance. In Switzerland, they had brotherly love, they had five hundred years of democracy and peace. And what did that produce? The cuckoo-clock!"'* (Orson Welles, giving his opinion of the Swiss in the film *The Third Man.*)

Sloanies Millions of them and yet not one person has ever admitted to being one. Caroline and Henry look set to be around for as long as Barbours are being manufactured. Currently known as **Fergies**. Will they go the same way as the Bourbons did in France, come the next revolution?

Blitz Kids Strange foppish types who used odd hair styles and make-up to cover acne-ravaged foreheads. Now virtually defunct, they spent their lives drinking orange juice in clubs with Gary Glitter and Elton John.

The Hollywood Brat Pack The main source of many a Sunday colour supplement article. 'Yeah we all drink Bud and appear in ninety per cent of Hollywood movies even though we haven't reached puberty yet and we're too young to vote.'

Ku Klux Klan To be pitied. Not only unable to spell, but also blighted with strange pointed heads and faces overrun with boils, since they always wear pillow-slips over their heads.

Yuppies and Yaps Young, up-and-coming aspiring urban professional persons who have yet to arrive at their destination. Cool people don't aspire. They inspire.

THE COOLS were born under four signs. *A word. A look. A movement. A silence.*

F I R S T   S I G N
A WORD

The words that go with cool are sometimes referred to as Cool-speak.

The Cools use words sparingly, even if their professions and occupations are connected with words. Cool journalists, TV script-writers, playwrights and novelists tend to favour the conversational exchanges of, say, *Waiting for Godot,* or *Edge of Darkness,* and selected dialogue from the method school of acting. Generally speaking, the fewer the words the better. When it comes to put downs, one-liners and verbal crucifixions, the Cools usually excel. The figures they would emulate (not their heroes mind you) would include Dorothy Parker, Winston Churchill, Oscar Wilde and Noël Coward.

THE DOROTHY PARKER
SCHOOL OF PUT DOWN

A former drama critic for *The New Yorker* magazine, Dorothy Parker hated pomposity and exaggerated social niceties. Following her example, replies in this section are occasionally harmless whimsy, but mostly they are intended to cut to the quick with rapier-like wit and cruelty. The recipient is usually the foolish asshole who is trying (seemingly successfully at first) to go one-up. Their moment is short-lived. They are quickly reduced to a quivering, blubbering mess while onlookers breathe a nervous sigh of relief, since they weren't the target of the venomous kick in the verbals.

When turning away a would-be suitor, an insurance salesman or a Jehovah's Witness, the Dorothy Parkerette would exclaim, loud enough to be overheard –

'Tell them I'm too fucking busy – or vice versa.'

For putting down another woman, Miz Cool is generally better qualified than Mr. Cool. Here are four examples –

'That woman speaks eighteen languages and she can't say no in any of them.'　　　　(DP)

'She (originally referring to Katharine Hepburn) *ran the whole gamut of emotions from A to B.'*　　(DP)

'Age before Beauty!'
(Clare Booth Luce being preceded through a door by DP who replied) *'Pearls before swine.'*

'She was the original good time that was had by all.'　　(BETTE DAVIS)

And let's not forget the classic shaft by Margot Asquith who, on a visit to Hollywood met Jean Har-

COOL

low the actress, who hadn't come across the name Margot before. Harlow asked whether the 't' in Margot was pronounced or not. 'No,' Miss Asquith replied 'the 't' is silent, as in Harlow.'

THE OSCARS

Oscar Wilde, the Irish author and dramatist, was a leader of the cult of art for art's sake. Apart from the excellence of his poems, short stories, and notorious private life, he was renowned for his brilliantly witty epigrams and repartee. Following a libel action he was imprisoned for two years for homosexual practices. He later proved with the *Ballad of Reading Gaol* that he could also cut the mustard when it came to serious writing. Here are a few examples of his wit –

Actress not noted for her looks: *'Mr Wilde, you are looking at the ugliest woman in Paris.'*
Oscar: *'In the world, madam!'*

To a gathering of close friends: *'There is only one thing in the world worse than being talked about, and that is not being talked about.'*

At the New York Custom House. *'I have nothing to declare except my genius.'*

On being told the cost of an operation: *'Ah, well, then, I suppose that I shall have to die beyond my means.'*

On his deathbed in 1900: *'Either this wallpaper goes, or I do.'*

THE WINSTON WAY

There was some truth in F. E. Smith's comment on old Winston when he said: *'Winston has devoted the best years of his life to preparing his impromptu speeches.'* Winston knew, along with other cool speakers, that whatever the put down, even though it sounds totally spontaneous, it often takes mucho preparation. Whatever the case, many of his famous replies sound like freshly squeezed curare –

Bessie Braddock MP: *'Winston, you're drunk. Horribly drunk.'*
WC: *'And you madam are horribly ugly. But I shall be sober in the morning.'*

Nancy Astor MP: *'If you were my husband I'd poison your coffee.'*
WC: *'If you were my wife I'd drink it.'* In later life, on being tactfully informed his fly was undone, he replied quite casually –
'Dead birds don't fall out of trees.'

Finally, there's a wonderfully whimsical quote attributed to a wounded ex-RAF pilot when asked in 1946 about the war: *'My dear the noise! And the people!'*

EAT YOUR HEART OUT NOËL COWARD.

25

COOLSPEAK

Coolspeak is not hipspeak, jive talkin', lovable cockney patois, Aussie speak or anything that has been commercially manufactured.

Coolspeak is usually quite a natural form of words that is not linked to any alternative colloquial dialects. Coolspeak operates on the principle of the smallest input to achieve maximum effective output.

Many verbal treatments have no place in the cool catalogue. **Impressions,** for example, are very uncool, even if you can take off David Frost ('*Hello, good evening and welcome*'), Basil Fawlty ('*For God's sake don't mention the war*') and Jimmy Greaves ('*Back of the net Saint, back of the net*'). Impressions of Yorkshiremen and Japanese people are plain embarrassing.

Impersonation or mimicry is allowable so long as it is correctly targeted and not overdramatic. (The Queen, apparently, is a great mimic and can take off heads of state with devastating effect.)

Foreign languages are cool. The more you know the better. But accents (frequently a problem for the aspiring English linguist) have to be reasonably impeccable. *Je suis un rock star, Ou est la plume de ma tante?* simply won't do.

Shakespeare quotations are questionable cool, since few beings can knock off the *To be or not to be* speech correctly without totally rewriting it.

Latin proverbs are cool –

cras amet qui nunquam amavit quique amavit cras amet

(A fabulous prize will be awarded to the first person who can name the source of this quote and offer a reasonable translation.)

UNCOOLSPEAK

Valley Speak A Californian derivative patented by Uncle Frank Zappa and his daughter. Examples –

Gag me with a spoon which roughly translated means 'I'm quite speechless with amazement', or *Grody to the max* ('quite awful actually') really grate and should have been allowed to perish along with *Hot Rats* and *Weasles Ripped my Flesh*.

Lovable Cockney Patois/Minderspeak Dreadfully uncool. Anyone who writes another lovable East-End series, TV or radio commercial better avoid this dead language or they might end up arrows. (Arrows in the head/dead.)

Jive Talkin' The product of too many *Shaft* movies. Even the brothers are jivin' less today. Examples –

Whatshakes bro? or *Whatshappenin' man?*
('Can you please tell me what is occurring?')

Slap 5
('I would like to shake hands with you in the form of pleasant greeting.')

Shitman that was wack
('Excuse me kind sir, but I must say that was a little sub-standard.')

A right bow-wow
('A reasonably unattractive female of the species.')

Mid-Atlantic Speak Bad enough spoken by the Americans but by other English-speaking nations it is quite unbearable. Examples –

Baby I like your style
('I don't know what else I'm supposed to say.')

COOL

I'm lagged
('I'm tired, as a result of some extensive flying I have recently undertaken.')

A strong wind chill factor
(cold).

A no-go situation
('This doesn't look as though it's going to work.')

Straight up with a twist
(A neat drink with a small peel of lemon/lime.)

An amazing sack artist
(Someone who excels at sexual athletics.)

Aussie Speak Once again, bad enough by the originals but as mimicry. . . Examples –

Cripes, I've had a skinful
('I'm sick.')

Strewth, time for a chunder
('I'm sick.')

Wacko-the-diddle-o, I feel proper crook
('I'm sick.')

Someone's stolen the 4X
('I think I'm going to be sick.')

A COMPENDIUM OF COOL AND UNCOOL WORDS AND PHRASES

THE COOL

Yes.
No.
M'n. (I'm thinking.)
Uh Huh. (Yes.)
Uh uh. (No.)
Goodbye. (ie forever, kid.)
Hello. (We've met before, but that was long ago and somewhere else.)
You drive.
Come here.
Get into bed. (I'm going to take a shower, so you better be ready when I come out.)
You shower. I'll watch. (I had a shower this morning.)
I have to make a call.
Pass the syrup.
I don't give a damn. (Rhettspeak.)
I haven't got long. (ie to live.)
There isn't much time. (ie before the shit hits the fan.)
I said I'd be back. (And now you're gonna pay.)
You'll be dead before I hit the ground. (I hope they buy that because I've just run out of bullets.)
Kick that piece over here.
Damn the torpedoes.
Nobody move.
Fuck yew.
Asshole.
So very tired.

We are all involved Dad. (Jimmy Deanspeak.)
It's just an old war wound.
The first one home buys the tea and buns! (Battle of Britainspeak.)
Shaken not stirred. (James Bondism.)

A little of this. A little of that. (In reply to the question 'what do you do for a living?')
Make a left.
Beam me up Scotty! (Attributed to an unknown defendant in the dock when asked if he had anything to say before the judge pronounced sentence.)

THE UNCOOL

Love it!
Right on!
Hey man.
Cheers! (meaning thank you.)

Unreal.
Far out.
Brill!
Triff!
Drop em!
I'd like to get into your pants. (A cool reply would be – sorry, there's already one asshole in there.)
Hung like a horse!
Vorsprung durch technik! (Referring to the male or female anatomy.)
Give 'er one for me.
Your place or mine?
I'll count till 3.
Back off!
Luscious Linda, Sizzling Sam, Curvy Corinne. (Sunspeak.)
Keep talking.
Fuck off. (As imaginative as giving a Max Bygraves record as a birthday present.)
Ogi-Ogi-Ogi. (The question.)
Oi-Oi-Oi. (The reply.)
You'll never walk alone!
Does the driver want a wee-wee?
It'll outdo your rust heap.
Tally Ho! (Hooray Henryspeak.)
Here's a song I wrote for a friend of mine. (Paul Ankaspeak.)
A loft in the village. (Yuppiespeak.)
Easy on the (tonic; barnet; bunny.)
C'est la guerre. (It's the only French I know.)
C'est la vie. (It's the only French I know apart from 'C'est la guerre'.)
Ay Up! (ie I can do impressions of Northerners.)

Who's farted? (as subtle as a flying mallet.)
Wanker!
Hang a right!
Enjoy!
Fake it till you make it.
It's not a chair; it's a piece of sculpture.
Get your people to call my people.
Let's burn plastic!
I know where you're coming from.
I hear what you're saying.
I'm trying to find myself.
It was a wonderful experience working with Misha (Baryshnikov). (Southbank Showspeak.)
I can't wait until I've enough money to fit my flat with low-voltage lighting.
Look after the pennies, and the pounds will take care of themselves. (Yawnspeak.)
Well out of order. (Sweeneyspeak.)
What's occurring? (Minderspeak.)
No way.
Pull up a pew, squire.
Let us retire to the nearest hostelry and partake of a few jars of foaming. . . (Camraspeak.)
All's fair in love and war. (ie I'm really a philosopher.)
Swings and roundabouts.
Look Sunshine.
OK Chief.
It's the business!

S E C O N D S I G N

A LOOK

'If looks could kill, they probably will' (PETER GABRIEL – Games without Frontiers)

The eyes. The mirror to the soul.
The eyes that lie.
Evil eyes, angel eyes, smiling eyes, Bette Davis eyes.
The eyes have it.
It's not necessarily handsome, not necessarily pretty, but the look is all electric. The look exudes nuclear magnetic attraction.

The look works on many levels, and in one glance synthesises optimism, unplumbed depths, anger, hatred, danger and amusement. Above all it communicates an overall sense of superiority. It can be one of rugged outdoors animalism or aristocratic civility. A crinkly smile scores points as does a practised scowl. Since the look alters with changes in fashion and with age, it is either improved by time or lost forever.

THEY LOOK

Terence Stamp (intermittent actor – Film Ref: Modesty Blaise. Far From the Madding Crowd. The Hit.)
Jean Shrimpton (Top Sixties model last seen running a Cornish hotel.)

Lee Van Cleef ('Angel Eyes' in *The Good, the Bad and the Ugly*.)
Alain Delon (French actor – Film Ref: *Borsalino. The Samurai*.)
Peter Murphy (The Bauhaus Man Ref: the Maxell Tapes TV commercial.)
Hugh Cornwell (the lean and hungry ex-schoolteacher and Stranglers lead singer.)
Brian Jones (ex-Rolling Stones guitarist. The scapegoat for the excesses of the Sixties.)
Robert Redford (actor – Film Ref: *The Candidate. The Natural*.)
James Dean (ex-actor – Film Ref: *Rebel without a Cause. East of Eden. Giant*.)
Jack Nicholson (the manic stare, the wicked eyebrows.)
Ingrid Bergman (Rick's chick from *Casablanca*.)
Isabella Rossellini (Ingrid's daughter – Top Model [Lancôme] at age 34.)
Montgomery Clift (ex-actor – Film Ref: *Raintree County*.)

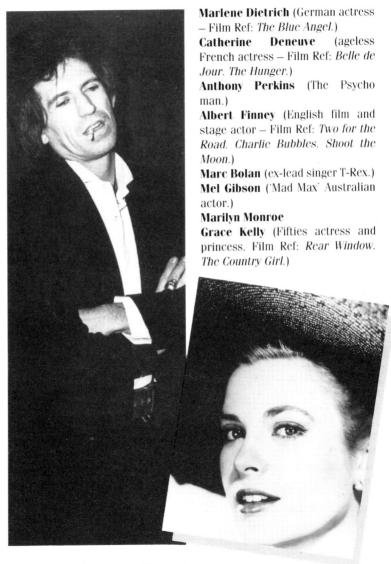

Keith Richard ('the world's most elegantly wasted human being'.)

Marlene Dietrich (German actress – Film Ref: *The Blue Angel*.)
Catherine Deneuve (ageless French actress – Film Ref: *Belle de Jour. The Hunger*.)
Anthony Perkins (The Psycho man.)
Albert Finney (English film and stage actor – Film Ref: *Two for the Road. Charlie Bubbles. Shoot the Moon*.)
Marc Bolan (ex-lead singer T-Rex.)
Mel Gibson ('Mad Max' Australian actor.)
Marilyn Monroe
Grace Kelly (Fifties actress and princess. Film Ref: *Rear Window. The Country Girl*.)

Rasputin (he may have hypnotised the Tsar and his family but that's as far as it goes.)

Steve Strange (the man who caused Revlon cosmetic share prices to go through the roof.)

General Zia of Pakistan (why does someone keep punching him in both eyes?)

Ken Livingstone (bought his moustache at the same place as Yasser got his beard.)

Yasser Arafat (bought his beard at the same place as Ken got his moustache.)

Charles Manson (helter skelter, harum scarum. His kind of looks could scare the large intestine out of the bravest junk-crazed mugger.)

Frank Zappa (so that's what too much LSD does for you.)

Yoko Ono (looking slightly better than when John first met her. Good thing about all round sunglasses tho' eh Yoko?)

W. C. Fields (no wonder he drank.)

Gracie Fields (no wonder she sang.)

Bernard Manning (just given birth to his sixth chin. It's the sort of joke he would've made.)

CAN SURGERY HELP?

It is possible to make your looks cooler without having to take desperate measures, eg wholesale plastic surgery or a head transplant. General tips like lose weight, drink less alcohol, eat healthier foods, live in Switzerland, may help – as can the following –

- Chew gum – builds up your jaw-line.
- Kiss more frequently – builds up your mouth.
- Dye your hair blonde – look what it did for Bowie, Sting, Billy Idol and Debbie Harry.
- Cap and polish your teeth – look what it did for the entire cast of *Dallas*.
- Experiment with facial hair – on young men beards are generally out but a couple of days' stubble will ensure a starring role in *Miami Vice*.
- Grow your eyebrows – look what it did for Margaux Hemingway and Brooke Shields.
- Get someone to put a cute little duelling scar on your face – a Douglas Fairbanks type, rather than one courtesy of Crazy Mick from Watford.
- Have a nose job – two if necessary.
- Pin your ears back – look what it did for Clark Gable.
- Avoid a hair transplant – it never helped Elton or Old Blue Eyes.
- Use make up creatively if you're a girl – if you're a boy remember what it didn't do for Steve Strange, Boy George and Divine.

THIRD SIGN

A MOVEMENT

The casual gestures, the insane gambles, succeeding against all odds, laughing in the face of danger, blows against the empire, the returned duelling slap, the knockout punch, the finger snap, turning around and walking away, riding into the sunset.

We've all seen them, we've all got our favourites:

George Raft – forever flicking a silver dollar into the air.

Indiana Jones – shooting the twirling sabre-man because he's too tired to fight the clean way.

Clint – only comfortable when he six-guns more than four people at a time.

David Carradine – performs slow-motion Kung-Fu when pushed just that little bit too far.

The saxophone player who plays on as the Titanic sinks.

The Fonz finger snap that gets the willing co-ed.

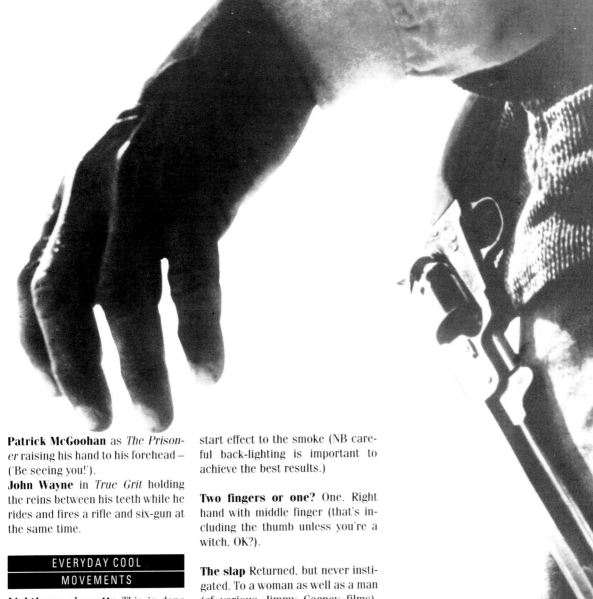

Patrick McGoohan as *The Prisoner* raising his hand to his forehead – ('Be seeing you!').

John Wayne in *True Grit* holding the reins between his teeth while he rides and fires a rifle and six-gun at the same time.

EVERYDAY COOL
MOVEMENTS

Lighting a cigarette This is done speedily and in one movement with the characteristic snap of a Zippo lighter. (See *Accessories*.)

Blowing the smoke An inhalation is followed by exhalation whilst talking, thereby producing a stop-start effect to the smoke (NB careful back-lighting is important to achieve the best results.)

Two fingers or one? One. Right hand with middle finger (that's including the thumb unless you're a witch, OK?).

The slap Returned, but never instigated. To a woman as well as a man (cf various Jimmy Cagney films). And to calm down the hysterical. (A good excuse to slap someone you dislike is to pretend they're hysterical.)

The grinding of the teeth Builds up tension.

The ordering of drinks From five rows behind the crowd, or simply using that old catchphrase 'the usual' (if the bastard mistakenly gives you a pint of lager, don't complain there and then, just waste him quietly on the way home).

The scribble in the air To indicate to waiters that you wish to pay the bill.

The raised gamble 'I'll cover that. And to make it a bit more interesting I'll up it another grand. No. Make that . . . five grand.' ☞

Pulling an ear Very Bogart. A sign that something is imminently about to happen.

The dropped fork at dinner Like hearing a pin drop, this is a very effective way of gaining attention. If that doesn't work try taking your glass eye out.

The strategic withdrawal on being surrounded by Chelsea supporters/Sandinista guerrillas Point to the sky in a kind of 'could that be Concorde?' way. If that fails, run like shit and later tell everyone you were just training for the next marathon. The old 'Beam me up Scotty' trick has been know to work one or twice, depending on the IQ level of your attackers.

F O U R T H   S I G N
A SILENCE

The unspoken word. The finger to the lips. Full of dark intent. Who are you? What's your name? Where do you come from? Let's keep them guessing with this one. Mum's the word.

Perhaps you're a woman with a ghastly secret? Your accent is worse than Lorraine Chase's? Or perhaps you're a handsome devil who's left with a permanent falsetto voice after doing too many impersonations of *'Sweet Child in Time'*.

You communicate through minimal movements. Flashing eye gestures. Spitting tobacco side-

ways. A shrug of the shoulders. The impatient tap of the foot. Since you're a man or woman of very few words, when you do actually say something it's weighed up very carefully.

Consider Marlon Brando and Maria Schneider in *Last Tango in Paris* meeting and then making prolonged love without speaking a word.

Watch Douglas Fairbanks, one of the silent movie kings, communicating through teeth and smiles and flashing gestures. (Well he had to, didn't he? They didn't have talkies in those days.)

Think about chess players, poker players and ultra-cool bidders at auctions.

Remember Clint. Silent. Most of the time.

WHAT TO DO IF SOMEONE ASKS YOU A DIRECT QUESTION

- Shoot them. ☛
- Ignore them.
- Grunt.
- Answer in a foreign language they can't understand.
- Take them into the bedroom before they can say another word.
- Give them your name, rank and serial number.
- Disappear through a strategically placed trapdoor which is operated by slight pressure applied to your left palm.

Growing Up With It

BABY COOL

When does cool begin?
When does it end?

From the cradle to the grave, or before birth and after death? From *Historical Cool* we know that cool reputations continue long after death. Many of the subjects already discussed have achieved immortal cool. They are up there with the Gods.

But what of little junior cool? Is it possible he can achieve a cool head start before he's born?

Certainly to ensure an advantage over other bratlets, it helps to have at least one beautiful and athletic parent and one incredibly bright one. Intelligent fathers and beautiful mothers are a good combination, as are athletic fathers and intelligent mothers. Mistakes, however, even with the right combinations, are possible. Take heed from George Bernard Shaw. A female correspondent trying to get better acquainted wrote to him saying *You have the greatest brain in the world, and I have the most beautiful body; so we ought to produce the most beautiful child.*

Shaw, hoping to avoid such a compromising situation, replied *What if the child inherits my body and your brains?*

EMBRYONIC COOL

- You've had a scan and you're found to be one of twins.
- You refuse to leave the womb after your nine months are up. *Come in and get me, doc!*
- You kick your mother in the stomach when she smokes.
- You make her sick when she drinks alcohol.
- You make her puke up when Daddy attempts a little rumpy-pumpy.
- You get her to sniff shoe polish and to demand large quantities of raspberry ripple ice-cream whenever you're in the mood.

THE BIRTH OF
THE COOL

Cool is born long before you become a virtuoso black trumpeter of the Miles Davis variety.

At birth you're perfectly formed, you've got hair, and you don't cry. As luck would have it, you've got all of Ma and Pa's best features.

You practise, from the word go, the four signs you were born under.
A word ☞ A howl.
A movement ☞ A dump.
A look ☞ Angelic, disguising mean intent.
A silence ☞ 'Give me what I want or I'll play dead.'

Baby Cool either walks and talks early, or walks and talks in his or her own sweet time. You gain attention by threatening to scream the house down (but you always hold back at the last moment, because one thing you've learnt is that grown-ups will be eternally blackmailed by the 'almost-scream').

You sleep all day so you can stay up all night with your Dad inhaling his Marlboro smoke and watching PG videos.

At Christmas you're especially sweet to Uncle Peter since you know he will spoonfeed you Rioja when no one's looking.

COOL

WHERE ONCE it was cool for eccentric rich parents to provide little master and miz with a private tutor (and occasionally in the case of little master a little ex-curricular tutoring in the form of a little mistress), nowadays school seems to be the order of the day.

The coolets will establish themselves early at whatever type of school they are sent to. (Cool does not differentiate between prep schools, comprehensives, grammars and public schools, except with respect to their slightly differing circumstances.)

Master Cool will be brought up on a diet of Molesworth, Captain Hurricane, Biggles, the Bash Street Kids, *Parade* and *Health and Efficiency* mags, and *Star Wars* videos. **Miz Cool** on under 14, 15, 16, *19* and *Over 21* magazines, the 4 Mary's, Irma Kurtz columns and Richard Gere videos.

■ **Master** will win at conkers, take his punishment like a man and be left unharmed by the school bully. Though essentially a loner, he will have a bespectacled sidekick called 'Fatty' who, despite being the butt of everyone's jokes, is exceedingly good at chemistry and, when he puts his mind to it, can make devastating explosive devices – the kind Libyans pay good money for.

■ **Miz Cool** will quickly achieve

hockey star status and be a school prefect, but will also smoke, drink and have more friends of both sexes than Mandy Smith in the lower sixth.

NB1 Both coolets remain aloof from teachers, but will make sure they get as many qualifications for as much fun and as little work as possible.

NB2 Those who find themselves at public school will be familiar with *If* and *Another Country*, so will know how to cope with some of its more cloistered aspects, eg avoiding uninvited buggery, taking care of swots, etc.

SCHOOL COOL AVOIDS

■ Joint Showers.

■ Vests.

■ Swots.

■ 'Teacher's pet' tags.

■ Crushes on other boys and girls.

■ Team spirit.

■ Crying.

■ Sniffing glue.

■ Unplanned pregnancy (ie getting into, or getting someone else into trouble).

■ Brand new bicycles.

■ Muddy puddles.

■ School dinners (as well as the more tacky variety encountered later in life in the Soho district).

■ Holding hands.

■ Chain-He.

■ Joint victimization.

■ Getting all hot and bothered over the Birds and the Bees.

■ Trainspotting and stamps.

■ Enid Blyton and Jennings.

■ Bunty and Judy.

SCHOOL COOL ENCOURAGES

Making money Running a book, charging duty-free mark-up on cigarettes, booze and sundry items, and 'fixing' – ie getting some bright spark to do homework or an exam for someone less bright, and charging ten per cent.

Reading Especially magazines like *Heavy Metal* – the illustrated science fiction comic from France, science fiction novels, Penguin modern classics, historical and political biographies, Marx, Freud, The Marquis de Sade and *Cider with Rosie*.

Being good at art Good for self-expression and for getting out of games, and for eventually getting into art school.

THE COMPLEET MOLESWORTH

GEOFFREY WILLANS & RONALD SEARLE

Computers Especially for the hacking possibilities in later life (eg bank frauds, Prince Philip's mailbox, etc.).

An appreciation of nature A lifelong cool characteristic, though it has to be played down to avoid appearing cissy.

Excelling at an unusual sport or pastime Fencing. Fives. Lacrosse. Judo. Seven Card Stud.

Languages Handy for school trips abroad and for communicating with les jeunes filles et garçons of various nations.

A WORD TO THE WISE

Since smoking, motorcycles, drugs, early sex, concert-going and movies of all types are easily experienced while at school, it's probably more difficult to be cool at school than at any other time.

School is best got through as quickly as possible, with the minimum of fuss and the maximum of education and qualifications. It's important to survive through to your next existence.

Remember, schools were always full of heroes who never actually made it afterwards.

Making a Career of it

THIS IS when the real education begins. The quicker you learn the quicker you survive. Later on, you'll speculate to accumulate (as *Daddy Cool* will tell you – plenty of readies makes for begetting even more readies). Right now it's time to accumulate so you can speculate (ie education is money). This is when the coolets make their first real decision in life.

They will either –

■ Cut their losses since they've got all the education they're ever likely to get.
■ Head for further education.
■ Head for an early career.
■ Head for the open seas.
■ Head for Daddy's millions.
■ Head for the dole as a last resort (see *Dole Cool*).

Having left school, master and little miz Cool finally achieve their Mr. and Miz status. Mr. Cool quickly realizes he'll probably have to work at something for the rest of his natural born life. Miz Cool realizes that she is entering a changing, but still sexist, society so she must work harder than her masculine counterpart to maintain a cool status.

THE RIGHT PATH

Art College A stepping stone to large Arts Council grants, exhibitions at the Tate Gallery, creating mindless electronic music for airports, or starting an arty band with a name like Roxy Music. Courses in video techniques, film and advertising are all recommended and David Puttnam will be more than glad to hear from you.

University/Poly Oxford or Cambridge preferably. After that, it doesn't really matter where. So long as it's not Hull. Do a quick three-year course, avoid MAs and PhDs, have a stupendous time, take a year off afterwards to travel around East Asia and generally get your act together. Face worklife refreshed and raring to go.

Conservation When the balloon finally goes up, and everyone's busy nuking the molecules out of each other, at least you'll be in some obscure Welsh conservationist backwater and will stand a better chance of conserving yourself. Remember, to survive is cool. (If

you're like Mel Gibson, radiation won't affect your good looks, and you'll get to star in a lot of your own real live road warrior pictures.)

The City Sloaney perhaps, capitalist definitely, but the City could be a quick means to an end, ie an East London riverside warehouse converted luxury home (see *Living With Cool*). If you're after a salary of £100,000 by age twenty-six, start here.

Greenpeace Exceptionally high tribal status. One of nature's last hopes. Not only do you get to see Nevada and fight the French once again, there's no family life whatsoever plus a very high stress rating.

Become a shop assistant in Los Angeles Generally punks and punkettes with diplomas in fashion graphics and interior design do well on Melrose Avenue and Rodeo Drive.

Hang around Universal Studios in Hollywood It worked for Errol Flynn, Burt Lancaster and David Niven.

Visit Uncle Dick in Hong Kong Who knows, you may even get to like each other. Either way he's probably loaded and looking for a tax loss.

Join MI5 Visit James at the old folks' home. Get natty little Exocet

briefcases from Q. End up in bed with a Russian intelligence colonel at the end of every caper.

Join MI6 Less glamorous. Get to make tea for George Smiley once in a while and file away a vital document under the wrong heading.

Work for Daddy Cool Especially if you've got no talent. The secretaries will be impressed and you might get to drive the Porsche once in a while when he gets legless at lunches at Langans.

Join the BBC/ITV If you are in embryonic form, apply now because it takes at least twenty years for them to process your application. Don't forget to pay your TV licence in the meantime, just in case.

Become a journalist Free trips. Free lunches. Self expression. Get to interview interesting people. Get on TV. Get famous.

THE WRONG PATH

Squat Not only does it sound like a bodily function, it invariably looks like the result of one. North London is particularly a no-go area. If you must squat, make sure you do it in extreme comfort, eg Belgravia — most senior Sloanes go abroad between May and April.

Join the Civil Service Unless, of course, you want to be Prime Minister. Civil servants fill dead men's shoes if they aren't dead already. The exceptions are the Foreign Office and the Treasury (all that treasure).

The Police Everyone knows someone has to do the job, but unless they can guarantee you *The Sweeney*, leave it out.

The Forces 'Yes, sir. No, sir. What's the point sir, since someone's already got their finger on the button sir?'

Go to a kibbutz Let them pick their own bloody oranges. Remember the next world war is likely to start in the Middle East.

Improve your grade of Hungarian 'A'-level You never needed it in the first place.

Go down the mines It may be cool to have a mining background – see virtually every Bryan Ferry interview – but leave mining to the professionals.

Work in a casino As a croupier you beat everyone but keep nothing, except the trashy imitation gold jewellery you received on your first day. The other side of the table is the place to be, 'wouldn't you agree Mistah Bond?'.

Become a poet

Write a novel Early days to attempt fiction unless you're a budding little Martin Amis (see *Cool Literature*). It'll take you forever and apart from Mills & Boon you won't find a publisher for stuff like this. 'I woke up to find Melissa, her golden blonde hair caressing the pillow like a ripened Botticelli. I decided that it was now or never to open the Valpolicella. But then I turned and saw the lurking TV detector van and all was plunged into darkness. . .'

Become a hippy The last one left for Katmandu in 1969. The ones that remained are now mostly successful antique and pine furniture dealers.

Become a Hari-Krishna devotee 'If you smile at me once more I'm gonna break all your teeth over three blocks of Oxford Street.'

Become an actor From RADA, to rep, to resting, to voice-overs for commercials. If you're serious head for Hollywood.

Take up a career in selling Little adverts in the *London Standard* offering £1,200 a week and free blow jobs, no experience necessary. Yes, we've all seen them. It's as unlikely as 'Miss Bond, Swedish massage' actually turning out to be a bona fide masseuse from Stockholm.

DOLE COOL

You can be cool anywhere. So you can be cool on the dole. How do the Cools cope with this increasing common but difficult phenomena, besides reading the collected works of Norman Mailer?

Write a book on your experience It'll either make a *Guardian* article, Channel 4 documentary, or it'll pass the time. Don't forget to throw in the odd murder, deviant sex angle and car chase.

Become a photographer's assistant All you have to know is how to load cameras, rearrange lighting, paint a studio, order pizza, and where to get booze after hours. You are then qualified to become a photographer's assistant and meet lots of lovely models of both sexes, go on photographic shoots to the Maldive Islands and after a while become a leading fashion photographer in your own right. No 'O' Levels needed but a beard helps.

Start a band Use your first credit card to buy a guitar before it's snapped up. Don't play any gigs. Get a mate called Martin from art college to make you a video. Borrow a tape of electronic airport music. Appear on *The Tube* dressed in black and last longer than Frankie Goes to Hollywood. 'Money for nothing and chicks for free'.

Become a model Whatever your shape, looks or age, tell people the dole look is the face of the Eighties.

Become an entrepreneur Join your local friendly government Enterprise Allowance Scheme.

Shoplift to finance larger projects Don't squander the money you make on the horses — instead invest it in every privatization or recent issue on the stockmarket (so far most have been amazing successes, eg British Telecom, British Aerospace, Laura Ashley, etc.). Then reinvest the money in carefully selected real estate and retire to the Caribbean.

Drive a cab A black one in English cities. A yellow one in New York. Emulate Robert De Niro in *Taxi Driver.*

Learn chess to a high standard You may never get to Russia but some games can last days.

Leave the UK You may never get to be a tax exile, but the world is a large place and opportunities exist everywhere if you know where to look for them. Besides, things often look better in the sun, even if you are down to your last 30 drachma and a bottle of yesterday's retsina. Visit Poland, Canada or Sweden if you want to discover how many other people are worse off than you.

WHAT TYPE of existence do Mr and Miz Cool lead when they're not on the streets? Where do they retreat to when the milk floats begin their rounds? When the police have given up the chase? After all, even the Ferrari needs to rest sometimes.

The Cools in fact spend quite a lot of their time at home. Their abode and the area they live in is actually very important to them though they'll rarely admit it. They prefer to let the home-base make its own understated statement.

The Cools' home is a reflection of their inner self. It's a great place for outsiders to pick up clues. The home turf is where Mr. and Miz Cool will mesmerize their audience with conspicuous ease.

Whatever it is, it's not a 'pad', a 'lair' or a 'den', but rather a sanctuary, a haven, a retreat.

Occasionally, house guests are invited to stay weekends. These are fairly fluid affairs where guests are left to their own devices for long periods but always come together at mealtimes, particularly dinner.

If the Cools have lovers, they have keys, but locks are frequently changed.

HEAVEN'S GATE

Some types of tenure are preferable to others, but all of them, in one way or another, have sufficient redeeming qualities to occupy the Cools.

NUMBER ONE
Rented Accommodation in town
If it's in Paris, it has a winding staircase, wooden shutters on the windows and boasts a concierge. The English equivalent, like the Roman, is more spacious and equipped with the most up-to-date gadgetry. In a big city it doesn't have to be situated in the best areas. A salubrious enclave – eg a nice part of Brixton or Toxteth, if one exists, will suffice.

The rent is ridiculously cheap since it hasn't been changed since the last owner died.

You rent –

a) Because like Bakunin you believe all property is theft.
b) Because you are a caged animal that doesn't want to be tied down.
c) You like to travel light since the nature of your everyday activities is so hush hush you could be called away at any time.
d) You can't afford to buy your own bloody place.

The landlord, if he's living, is always abroad. When he returns on those occasional visits it's always at least forty-eight hours after you've given the mega-party to end all mega-parties and you've just time to glue his priceless vase collection back together again.

TRANSPORT – Since you're probably saving on the readies you can go totally OTT with an AC Cobra (see *Auto Cool*).

NUMBER TWO
The Hotel (City Centre)
Ideal for rock stars, recluses, ageing actors and actresses and the odd cat burglar. Here we are talking *Grand Hotel* and not the 200 motels lot of the support band, or the continuous Holiday Inn hangover of the itinerant salesman.

You have your breakfast in bed, you leave your valuables in the safe, and your laundry, shoe-shining and pressing all in the charming hands of an army of lackeys. You get your tennis lesson from the professional who says your service is coming on nicely.

If you're with the 'Big Band' the chances are the management will nervously have cordoned off three floors for your entourage, and you'll probably be creating your own entertainment. Apart from an endless round of free-for-all post-gig parties, fun things to do include setting off fire extinguishers, throwing TV sets out of windows and flushing ignited sticks of dynamite down the bog.

TRANSPORT Limos and taxis. No personal transport.

NUMBER THREE
Paid up or mortgaged flat/house
The size and space occupied under this category should be offset by the area you live in. There's nothing cool about having a six-bedroom house in urban hicksville when you could be in a neat little two-bedroom flat in the heartland of things.

A garden would be nice or at least a balcony. After all, even if you only get 4½ days a year sunshine, your urban tan will require attention.

A view is important, too. Not the local steelworks but the sky, the sun and the distant rolling hills. This is the place you really invest your cool in, so look ahead to *At Home With Cool* for the right interior decoration.

TRANSPORT Jaguar Mk. 2 3.8 litre. Volkswagen Beetle.

NUMBER FOUR
The Studio/The spacious Attic/ The Warehouse
By the river in a smart complex. Or in an undisturbed, unvisited, semi-deserted wasteland. The ace-cool frog in *Diva* had one. Faye Dunaway

had one in the *Eyes of Laura Mars*. The upmarket city-whizz-kid elite are snapping them up, so are photographers and amateur movie makers. The walls are all white, the pipes are all bare. Brick and blocks are held together by a whole Pilkington factory of glass. The couches are comfortable, the photographs are all black-and-white. The view is of the whole city. You practise standing by the window muttering 'I love this dirty town . . .'

TRANSPORT A Citröen Light 15, any Ferrari, Lamborghini or Maserati.

NUMBER FIVE
The Cottage in the Country
The fast set-up for weekends. Lazy local hostelries, long breezy walks. Ideal for the novelist, the painter, the best-of-both-worlds-towny.

Look to Dorset, Hampshire, Gloucestershire, Oxfordshire, Kent, Cornwall or the Cotswolds.

Plenty of old wood panelling, over-grown gardens, four-poster beds, mahogany sideboards and optimistic *bonhomie* at dinner. No hippies, vegetarians or active Labour Party militants.

TRANSPORT Old Alvis, Aston Martin DB 4, 5 or 6.

N U M B E R   S I X
The broken down Farmhouse
Just scraped enough credit together for a bank loan for this one after you fell in love with it one summer after taking the wrong road back to the city. Ideal for Cool Couples. Different from No. 5 *The Cottage*, as the overall look is more broken down and there are no available readies for repairs. Muddy boots, old clothes and sweaters, frequent wood fires, large teapots in even larger kitchens, plenty of animals – dogs, sheep and horses – and the odd watercolour.

This time the fast set are not so fast, and are more the outdoors type – fishing, chopping wood, blasting tin cans with old shotguns.

TRANSPORT Battered old station wagon, with an old 2CV or Renault 5 as a second car. A rarely used track bike. But no old hay-covered Rolls in the barn. Those are strictly for real farmers.

N U M B E R   S E V E N
A combination of 3 and 5 or 6
Having two existences or more, like several identities, is cool. Keep them guessing. 'Why are the Cools never around at weekends? Is there something going on I don't know about?' 'Why don't the bastards ever invite me down to lousy old Cookham?'

TRANSPORT The Beaulieu Classic Car Collection. A Tiger Moth bi-plane in the hangar. A hot-air balloon.

N U M B E R   E I G H T
A cottage in Hampshire.
A Town House in Regents Park.
An appartment in New York. A villa in Bali-by-Sea. An option on a space station.

TRANSPORT Helicopter. Yacht. Ocean-going Liner. Boeing 707. Lear Jet. Hydrofoil. Space Shuttle, etc.

AT HOME WITH COOL

The last thing you notice about the Cools' home is that it simply oozes disgustingly outrageous good taste.

Whatever it's got, you can't get it from Conran, Hicks, Heals or Harrods. There's no way it was inspired by *Interiors* or helped by *House and Garden*. It's an original creation, pure and simple.

It's full of light and space. It's full of comfort and white walls with dashes of low-key colour. It's full of slowly unravelling surprises that only become apparent after the eye has discerned the ease with which old furniture sits with the new, foreign objects blend with domestic ones.

In the organized chaos that is the Cools' home there is a sense of peaceful order. It puts the outside world to shame. It makes you want to emigrate inside.

As a guest of the Cools, you will be allowed to explore and

satisfy your curiosity. As a Cool you delight in deliberately but passively encouraging the curious with clues and unfinished puzzles –

The locked room. The wardrobe filled with a stranger's clothes. The paintings and drawings stacked neatly against the wall. The unfinished chess game. The buddy-buddy 'me-Arnie and Schlitz' type photographs that are seen everywhere, full of unknown faces and exotic locations: With Hem at Key West. With Sigourney on the set of *Alien*. With Sting on someone's yacht in Barbados. And one with the Princes of Wales that hangs in the loo.

Your eye takes in an extensive record collection, an extensive catalogued video collection, an extensive library with its fair share of first editions, some objets d'art from Papua New Guinea and Ultima Thule, and various battered old stringed instruments.

Money has been spent but by no means on everything.

Most of the financial damage has been done by the carpets, curtains, wallpaper, a couple of large, fat, puffy sofas, a bed and the hi-fi systems.

Least money has been spent on the kitchen (appliances are random), the bathroom which is small and functional (but does boast one of those skin-peeling super showers) and other items of furniture.

The expensive paintings are heirlooms. The watercolours were gifts from the artist.

Limited edition lithographs are thin on the ground since they go out of fashion so quickly. There are no framed posters, or homage of any kind to a public hero.

ROOM BY ROOM
BY ROOM

The Games Room Complete with a full sized snooker table. 'Remember that night when Eric, Rod and Jeff came round for the post-gig party? The chicks got right miffed 'cos we wouldn't let them play with us. Heh, heh.'

The Dark Room In the cellar for photographic development. Next to the cobwebbed wine and port racks.

The Attic The attic houses amongst other treasures a camera obscura which has the ability to scan the whole neighbourhood and its inhabitants for approximately half a mile radius. Confused? Then see the Powell and Pressburger film *A Matter of Life and Death*.

The Conservatory Bright, white and peaceful. Full of tropical plants, rare orchids and canaries. You drink tea out of china cups as you sit on wicker chairs being interviewed by Alan Whicker.

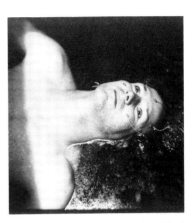

The Cellar An isolation tank designed by John Lilly, doyen of isolation tank introspection (see the Ken Russell film *Altered States*) for rest, relaxation and travelling back in time.

The Music Room 24-track recording. Various instruments and taped synthesized sounds. Drum rhythms from around the world. Eno at the controls putting the finishing touches to your long awaited first solo album.

The Bedroom Light, tidy and stark. Bare floorboards are covered by a tiny rug. The bed is large and rests no more than two feet above the ground. There's one picture, one lamp, one book, one glass of water, one box of tissues and one radio. Nothing else, not even a wardrobe or a blister pack of contraceptive pills.

The Living Room A fireplace. Wide open and brick. Odd metal hanging bits from ancient blacksmiths are stuck into the surrounding wall. Somewhere there's a rocking chair. The only real luxury that instantly catches the eye is a baby grand piano.

The Kitchen A Krups home electric expresso machine. The odd hint of *Joseph Pour La Maison*. A Welsh dresser, a real one, not one made of Barnes-cloned-pine, on which is resting a motley collection of old Delft blue and white plates. A washing machine. A dryer. A dishwasher. But no freezer or microwave oven.

The Toilet/Bathroom A Victorian cast iron bath with original brass attachments. A toilet with a wooden seat. A couple of large Eileen Gray bathroom mirrors to create a feeling of space. Cosmetics and toiletries are everywhere. There are no books or magazines – so as to discourage the 'marathon-dumper'. And no bidets – to discourage a permanently occupied bathroom. A large bamboo bin takes care of those empty Bollinger bottles. Small stereo loudspeakers are connected to the master system and carefully camouflaged in the wall.

Other clues
- A sprinkling of Art Nouveau and Art Deco mirrors, lamps, oils and figurines. Three or four Richard Sapper Tizio lamps for desks and bedside reading.
- A framed caricature by Ralph Steadman or Gerald Scarfe.
- A signed Helmut Newton or Norman Parkinson (the former of a distinctly dark de Sadian dolly, the latter a cigarette-holdered social climber of the early Fifties).
- A black Forties Heiberg tele

phone in the bedroom. A wall telephone in the kitchen. Your number has an ex-directory listing which is changed every month. An Ansaphone with a coded message or jingle sung by Paul McCartney.
- A compact disc player.
- A Dansette record player for playing those old scratched 45s.
- A cleaning lady with a heart of gold. (Not one of those youthful layabouts who just want to clear out your larder and your booze cabinet.)

COOL PETS

Ferrets. Shire horses. Turtles. Seals. Rumble Fish. Kangaroos. Bats. Lemmings. Koala Bears. Dolphins. Dormice. Dogs (especially Sharpies)

UNCOOL PETS

Cats. Budgies. Crocodiles. Piranahs. Fish. Hyenas. Camels. Bunnies. Goldfish. Hawks. Doves. Hamsters. Parrots. Tortoises. Albatrosses. Minks. Baby Elephants. Panthers.

THE UNCOOL HOME
INSTANT ALARM BELLS

- Miniature horse-drawn window boxes – neigh lad.
- A wall safe behind a painting – somewhere to keep the pools coupons, the Greek stamp collection and the foreign coins.
- Constable/Turner prints with lacquered gold fabric frames.
- Crossed knives, guns, swords, bazookas, pistols.
- A green lady by Tretchikoff.
- Spanish dancers on the mantlepiece.
- Tiger skin/bear skin rugs – real or imagined.
- Yellow-gold/green-gold satin Barbara Cartland drapes.
- Yellow-gold/green-gold sofas or ones made of ersatz leather.
- Red satin.
- Net curtains.

- Fluorescent lamps.
- Track lighting.
- Interior designed indoor pillars and arches – *so* Roman Empire. *so* Empire Stores.
- A jacuzzi – *so* Victor Lownes. *so* unhygienic.
- Crinolines on the bog roll.
- A bidet with gold painted taps.
- A stuffed dogfish or favourite deceased poodle in glass display box.
- A bar that's built round pirate barrels, with gin, rum, Irish, sherry labels.
- Cheap Woolies decanters with silver I.D. dogtags.

- Imitation gaslog/coal fires.
- Dogs with nodding heads.
- Imitation brick paper. 'Oo, dun it look real!'
- Imitation tile paper. 'Oo, you'd never know the difference.'
- Electronic family organ with drum machine. 'It's so simple you can play it with two hands, one hand, no hands.'
- A Wurlitzer organ that rises out of the floor with your host at the keyboard.
- The Country Diary of an Edwardian Lady.

In fact, anything that might turn up on The Price is Right.

To recap, the cool home has: No rubbish. No tat. Nothing quaint or bijou. No Torremolinos. No Argos. No Frankie Vaughanos.

No Silver trophies of any kind (for excellence at squash, badminton, 'beating-off', etc.).

No professional acclamations 'To our good friend J.B. Smith, Top Sales Rep. 2nd Class – from all of your chums at the Hull Area Managers Office. Keep up the good work.'

No framed degree certificates from Oxbridge or Luton Poly.

SHOPPING AROUND

Shopping is essentially a bore and a chore. If you have to do it (i.e. can't get some schmuck to do it for you) go out heavily disguised. Black glasses, scarf, hat, long high-collared trenchcoat. Like an incognito Jackie Onassis wandering around Manhattan.

If someone recognises you in W.H. Smith, put your copy of *Amateur Photographer* back on the rack and pretend you're tailing someone in the interest of national security.

Never shop on a Saturday. If you spend more than 4.2 minutes looking for a parking space, give up and go home. Better to park on a yellow line than to walk. But it's highly uncool to get a ticket – another dilemma the Cools just have to skate around. Try Thursday night shopping to be on the safeway side.

Drink

THE COOLS like their drink but they aren't alcoholics, piss artists or lushes.

They can drink to their hearts' content but rarely get drunk. If on rare occasion they do, it's not to crawl around in the gutter with a case of the *Apocalypse Now* helicopters, or try to talk to God on the great white telephone. Mr. Cool is more likely to take the guise of an endearing Robert Redford out of *The Way We Were* doing a little boy lost act as he passes smiling into sleep. Either that or a bitter Bogart resplendent in white tux, quietly demolishing the contents of a bourbon bottle and countless Luckies as he wonders why of all the gin joints in all the towns all over the world, she had to walk into his.

Miz Cool, like Karen Allen in *Raiders of the Lost Ark*, can usually drink anyone under the table if called to do so, be they Mongolian traders, Irish poets or High Plains Drifters. She will, however, suffer from hangovers just like anyone else.

Some Cools don't drink at all. The hero in *Absolute Beginners* doesn't. How does he get by? Simple, he gets his kicks from himself. You either drink a lot, or not at all he explains: 'Liquor's not made for zips, but for orgies or total abstinence. Those are the only wise weddings between man and bottle.'

The Cools harbour a deep seated fear of ending up like W.C.

Fields, Oliver Reed or distant aunts with their secret supplies of hidden gin bottles. They want their faces, particularly their noses, to remain completely intact as they grow old gracefully. For this reason the Cools can be seen to demonstrate traces of nervousness and uncontrolled fidgeting when the cheapo port is wheeled out at dinner parties.

The Cools believe more in the art of drinking and its enjoyment rather than going for quantity and oblivion. They'll drink their frozen akvavit down in one, from little one-shot glasses, but they won't do the same to their pints.

COOL TIPPLES

Champagne The Cools like champagne but not all the time and not necessarily the best. Nevertheless a reasonable part of their drinks budget goes on the fizzy stuff. The Cools look for little bubbles and plenty of them. Ice cold and from expensive, preferably crystal, receptacles (flutes).

NON VINTAGE – Bollinger. Philliponat. Sainsbury's.

VINTAGE – Bollinger R. D.. Louis Roederer Cristal. Clos de Goisses. Taittinger Crémant Blanc de Blancs.

The champagne ritual touches on much of what the Cools do. Any excuse: Sunday morning shower and champagne. The 'let's forget the Porsche being written off

and have a bottle' occasion. And the 'I know we're the guests of honour at this charity reception and Bob, Paula, Mick and Jerry and David will be there, but we can see them any night of the week'.

Kir Sirop de Cassis with a good quality white wine, preferably Burgundy. (Generally Cassis will enhance the taste of the cheapest wine.)

Kir Royale Preferably *à la mure*, which enhances the taste of fresh mulberries blended with the lightness of good champagne. If in doubt try it at one of the very best authentic Paris family restaurants – Le Vieux Bistrot, 14 Rue de Cloitre, Notre-Dame, 4C.

Chilli Vodka Stick three large chil-

lis in a bottle of Stolichnaya. Wait two months and you'll have a Bloody Mary that'll brighten up even the darkest day.

Dry Martini Preferably as suggested by James Bond in *Casino Royale*. 'Three measures of Gordon's, one of vodka, half a measure of Kina Lillet. Shake it very well until it's ice cold, then add a large thin slice of lemon peel. Got it?.'

Malt Whisky The Macallan. Laphroaig.

Sherry If you must, let it be San Patricio.

Port Good vintage stuff, most houses. Recent good years 1963, 1966, 1970 and 1977. Dow's,

Taylor's, Fonseca, etc. Only to be drunk when it's time, so leave the 1977 in the cellar, OK?

Cognac Hennessy X.O.

Armagnac Any, since a willingness to take it on shows class.

Pimms We all know about No. 1 cup, but the Cools are well versed in concoctions containing Pimms No. 2 through to No. 57 cup varieties.

Wine A little knowledge goes a long way but there's no need to be fanatical. The Cools understand that most wines, even white wines, need to breathe and that sediment takes a long time to settle. Wine is decanted by deft hand or muslin. The Cools don't spend big bucks just for a fancy name. They like to experiment too.

Red BORDEAUX: First class growth clarets. 1959, 1961 especially and later 1966, 1970 and 1975. Château Lafite, Château Mouton Rothschild, Château Latour. A special recom-

COOL

mendation for Pétrus, the top wine of the Pomerols. Other good class growth clarets. Château Canter-merle and Montrose.

BURGUNDY: Good years 1961, 1964, 1966, 1971. Chambertin, Bonnes-Mares, Richebourg, La Romanée, La Tâche. A good shipper is impor-tant in this category.

OTHERS: Dão (Portuguese). Amarone (Italian). Campo Fiorin (Italian). Good Rioja (Spain). Château Grillet (French). Côte Rôtie (French).

Dry white ALSACE: Pinot, Reisling, Gewurztraminer.

BURGUNDY: Corton Charlemagne. Good years 1964, 1967, 1969, 1971. OTHERS: Muscadet sur Lie.

Sweet white Sauternes (Château Yquem) and Barsac.
Beerenauslese and Eiswein.

Beer Cold, bottled and preferably superior Dutch, German or Belgian brews. Retain the small continental head on the glass even though it's not the English way. Sip slowly.

Beer Cold, canned – your old ladys' just moved out. You've had a hard day at the precinct? Then rip the lid off a Budweiser, fresh from the fridge.

Guinness Pints of draught in Guin-ness mugs. Drunk in the same slow style as the characters from Seven-ties commercials.

UNCOOL TIPPLES

Pints of lager Follow the bear and follow the sleep. Generally is not cool to drink pints, or halves, of lager as it equals instant demotion to Boy Racer, Jack-the-Lad, wally status. The worst offender is night-club lager, ie flat throughout and served in plastic glasses.

The wrong wine
MOUTON CADET The 'apprentice-sheep' of white wines found in most off-licences.
HIRONDELLE It may not be duff, but it's hardly a palette pleaser.
NIERSTEINER The German version of Valpolicella.
VALPOLICELLa The Italian version of Niersteiner.
LAMBRUSCO The Coca Cola of wines.
CHIANTI Even if you are having the Corleones around to dinner.
AUSTRIAN WINES Suivez the pissed.
LIEBFRAUMILCH Especially the Blue Nun variety.
CARDBOARD BOX WINES Don't go with tastebuds.
ANTIFREEZE WINES Don't go with kid-neys.

The wrong champagne
MOËT & CHANDON.
DOM PERIGNON.

The wrong port
COCKBURNS.

The wrong malt
GLENFIDDICH.

The wrong brandy
MARTELL or anything with a picture of Napoleon on it. The Cools know that Cognac is brandy, but brandy isn't Cognac.

Cocktails Like exotic ice cream dishes, the highly strung fellows of the Harvey Wallbanging brigade, with few exceptions, are strictly uncool even if you are in rio de Janeiro, Spetsai or Studio 40002. The Cools can't take Slow Screws up against the Wall seriously, nor Flying Lizards, Dacquiris or Dead Bears straight up with a twist. Tequila Slammers epitomize some of the worse aspects of Brits abroad. 'Set 'em up Georgio . . . burp . . . one, two, three . . . dahn in one! Come on you blues . . . !'

G&T, whisky and american or soda. Bloody Marys, Dry Martinis and one or two others, though essentially cocktails are OK since they've done their time and they aren't fussy.

As a rule, the Cools don't like cocktails and that's all you need to know.

Yards of ale Gallons of sick.

50

THE COOLS have slightly ill-defined ideas about cooking and food. They love giving dinner parties, love going to them, but with the exception of the odd cool master chef (amateur or otherwise), the Cools take little pleasure in cooking. Eating *chez eux* is generally a means to an end – six chops, a sack of potatoes and four Angel Delights and hunger has been assuaged.

The Cools like eating out, whether it's in the best restaurants or in greasy spoon cafes. Even the smoking and drinking Cools who are minimalist in their approach to food share an equal interest in the ambience of restaurants. They simply substitute starters and desserts for an extra carafe of wine and double Remy rations.

The Cools like TV dinners. Take aways. Bubble and squeak. Baked beans and barbeques.

Junk food they can take or leave, and usually do.

Miz Cool is good at making home-made pizza the diameter of a baseball pitch and she can knock up a quick soufflé if she puts her mind to it.

Mr. Cool makes an excellent Sunday morning breakfast. He's a dab hand at roasting chicken (bung it in the oven, John) but is a bit concerned when it comes to beef (three hours for every 2 lbs, plus twenty minutes for every cubic centimetre of oven space – that makes twelve days in all).

Boiling an egg The exact time of 3 minutes 51 seconds is achieved by boiling the egg for the duration of Dire Straits *Down to the Water Line.*

Chopping onions Wear a snorkel mask like the central character in *Diva.*

Tagliatelli and other pasta dishes Carefully remove Marks and Spencer wrapping and put in oven. Take out after half an hour. Put in saucepan and re-heat, since it's still frozen in the centre.

Toasting bread Put bread in the toaster. Pluck toast out of air when cooked. Alternatively put under grill, and finish your bath. Take out burnt toast and replace with fresh slices, this time watching over it.

Spices Fresh black pepper carefully grated and dispensed liberally.

Sauces Yesterday's left over Rioja mixed in with a bit of mild cheddar

grated. Heinz tomato ketchup. English (no foreign) mustard.

Chilli The hotter the better.

Vichysoise Pour yourself a glass of Vichy water while waiting for the delicatessen to deliver a large bowl of the stuff for your very select dinner party.

Peanut butter and jelly sandwich Take two slices of thick white bread. Spread butter on one side followed by jam/marmalade or honey. Spread only peanut butter on the other side (liberally), and then shut carefully. Eat standing up.

Peanut butter, lettuce and mayonnaise on white toast As above, but with different ingredients and toasted (see *Toasting bread*).

Baked beans Only Heinz will do. Add worcestershire sauce and stir carefully. Serve with smoked salmon on thinly sliced pieces of buttered brown bread.

Special occasion cornflakes First take Kelloggs cornflakes and empty into a bowl. Follow with gold-topped milk – ice cold and creamy. Chop strawberries in quarters and arrange carefully over flakes – spread a little caster sugar. Put on a tray with red rose, orange juice, a little toast and some Greek yoghurt.

(Tell her you're sorry you got pissed last night, and it'll never happen again.)

Late night surprise The Cool couple return home from the Academy Awards or some opening night bash. Whichever one has showered that day prepares a tray of kedgeree, kippers, Indian tea, digestive biscuits and Brie. They invariably fall asleep before they can eat it, but sometimes have it cold for breakfast.

Potatoes Whatever else, the Cools really like their potatoes. Here are some exciting recipes:

MASHED POTATOES Peel, boil, butter, mash, milk, mash, onion, mash, stick sausages in liberally the Dennis the Menace way and serve with pleny of Old Nick rum and Diet Coke.

SAUTÉED POTATOES Boil a bit. Chop up in slices or cubes. Cook in butter and oil.

BAKED POTATOES Stick in oven for an hour or two, or until they look done.

CHIPPED POTATOES (or Chips) Buy some from the fish and chip shop, ideally cooked in dripping not oil. Separate from the fish and eat.

POMMES (ie Potatoes) DAUPHINOISE Slice raw potatoes thinly. Lay in buttered dish. Pour over heated milk and single cream with added garlic and spices. Grate some cheese. Cook in oven for about an hour.

CROQUET POTATOES Take out of the packet, stick in oven or deep fry in oil.

FRIED POTATOES Half boil, chop up, fry in 50/50 olive oil and butter. Like sautéed potatoes really but with a different name.

POMMES DUCHESSE Make up some mashed potato. Add egg yolk and seasoning. Put in a piping bag and pipe out like whirls. Put in oven for short time and bake till golden brown.

ROAST POTATOES Half boil, stick in the oven with roast.

THE COOLS AREN'T VERY KEEN ON THE FOLLOWING

'Who's turn is it to cook tonight?'

'I cooked last night so it must be yours.'

'I've invited Mr. Big Bastard Client and his wife over for dinner tonight and I know it's short notice but, as my job is more important than yours, pick up the groceries and hoover the flat.'

Earl Grey tea Everyone makes such a fuss about it when in reality it's like Watneys.

Raw carrots Especially the big fat ones and the keen folk with perfect white teeth like Robert Redford who pretend to like them.

Microwave ovens 'Very hot I grant you but my sprouts are still raw.'

Salt mountains by the side of the plate 'You'll find there's already two truckloads of Saxa in the goulash.'

People who leave half their food
Q. 'Why not just take half in the first place?'
A. 'Because they'd probably leave half of that.'

Sugar Especially in tea, coffee and sandwiches.

Sushi (the Jap variety). The Cools actually like it but can't bear the way people go on about it, so they don't bother.

Lobster Bubble bubble. Squeak squeak.

Veal

Vegetarian (Some Cools are almost total vegetarians but they haven't managed to give up the bacon sarnies yet.)

Kebabs (the takeaway variety). Why? Because I've only got sixty-seven feet of intestine and I intend to hang on to all of it.' NB doner kebabs are now recognized as the principal cause of food poisoning.

Custard with skin Sends shivers up the spine.

Nouvelle Cuisine I could eat six courses and still be starving.

Designer chocolates.

Decaffeinated coffee.

Spinach croissants.

Designer lettuce ie mâche, radic-cio, feuilles de chêne.

Turnips If you can't get out of eating these at a dinner party wear your snorkel mask to dampen the taste and armpit aroma.

AUTO COOL

Bootleggers in long black limos. Curtains dancing to the tune of Thompson machine gun fire. Formula One Cinzano-drinking racing drivers sporting Oyster Perpetuals. Insane car chases down the slopes of San Francisco that end in the destruction of two shopping malls and an oil refinery. *Duel, Vanishing Point* and many a buddy-buddy road movie. Classic cars in mint condition driven by the likes of James Bond: the silver Aston Martin DB5 with every known accessory to fight the bad guys (ejector seats, changing number plates, machine guns, oil slicks).

Pre-Jap bikes. Steve McQueen's almost great escape. *The Getaway. The Sweeney.* The *Diva* hero with a matching pair of white Citroën Light 15 Tractions. Getting your kicks on Route 66 with only a clean pair of Levis and a packet of Lucky Strikes. Coast to coast confidence. Cruising. Driving slow. The Cars. Burning rubber. Screeching tyres. Parking à la Parisienne (ie sideways to the pavement).

Whatever else cool is, wheels are somehow connected to it. No-one ever got round L.A. without a car. No-one ever got round Sigourney without a car.

Even if the sum total of your road excitement was passing your test, doing a ton up the M1, or giving

chase to a Fiat Panda because it was probably slower than your Moggy Minor, the Cools agree that some form of wheels are essential.

The Cools also agree that there will be occasions when it's better to walk, although the occasion has yet to arise.

The Cools are cautioned from an early age to the wrong lumps of tin. In fact so strongly do they feel about some mechanical monstrosi-

ties they ensure that offending ones are banished from their street. This is done by bribing breaker's yards to tow them quietly away while their owners are asleep.

THE I'D RATHER WALK COLLECTION

These are the ones that adhere to the cult of the funny sticker. The Kevin and Sharon partnership, the pre-pubescent Playboy Club member. The ones that pay homage to Capital Radio with stickers that blot out the sun. The ones with such sticky witticisms as 'My other car's a Datsun', 'Limbo dancers bend over backwards to do it', and so on.

Their heroes are *Starsky and Hutch*, the *Dukes of Hazzard* and *Night Rider*. Wide wheels, bucket seats, furry dice, air fresheners and spoilers rub shoulders with go-faster stripes, personalized number plates, Van Halen Live, and CB radio.

A lifetime's ambition is to put a Porsche engine into a Beetle.

Death Race 2000, Smokey and the Bandit and *Convoy* are great films. As for crashing and drunken driving? What's all the fuss about.

Among the most egregiously uncool makes –

Morris Marina (Any model) The model 'T' Ford re-incarnated. Unfortunately, though appearing to be

Austin Maestro The car that talks back. Its petrol and mileage gauge changes upwards of sixty times over a two hundred yard stretch. Mr. and Mrs. Exceptionally-Sensible go and visit their in-laws in this one.

Vauxhall Chevette A supermarket trolley with lights. The designer was obviously going through a marriage break-up.

Ford Capri (any model) The debate has long existed over this one. Sharon and Kevin fundamentally disagree. It was the clincher that brought them together after their computer date. It runs on lager, crisps, wide collars, gold chains and high heels.

Ford Sierra The salesman's delight. The idea came from several low budget SF movies of the Fifties. Is it really a car, or a nuclear fallout shelter for the household pets?

Porsche 944 The 924 with spoilers – these cars take the meaning literally. Like Britt and her toyboys, this one is for managing directors of newly-begun companies who can't quite see themselves in the right car for their age.

Renault Gordini The Renault 5 – no problem. The Renault Turbo – fat, but endearing. Le Car était OK. Mais ça monstrosité?

held together with string and Smarty tubes, these are built to last.

Austin Allegro (Any model) Inspired by the Noddy vehicle (but at least Noddy's was a sports car) it's difficult to tell which end is which. Even little old ladies have been known to gob on this one.

Volvo Estate In appearance it looks as if it was designed by the German Panzer company. The stress on hyper-safety (the sidelights are eternally switched on) give its owners an air of superiority Charles I would've been proud of. Particularly risqué are the ones with lawn-mowers in the back for doing the country house garden at weekends. The Volvo advertising agency should be sentenced to a

good many hours community service for their beautifully endearing advertisements.

Cortinas Mk 1 thru 15 The football supporter's dream. The Saturday cruiser. Capital Radio stickers and coloured scarves adorn the windows up the M1 en route to Manchester.

Datsuns (all models, even the sports varieties) Invariably sooty, invariably without brake-or sidelights. The slowest motorized transport on the road, their drivers are forever in search of bingo halls and sales at Millets. These cars are incapable of differentiating one lane from another. Small wonder the company changed their name to Nissan.

Fiat 127 'I pulled up in front of the Beverly Hills Hotel to pick up Kelly. For some strange reason she appeared not to recognize me.'

Austin Princess A wedge of cheese on wheels. Designed by the same guy who was going through the marriage crisis. Or was it the one who designed Tower Hamlets?

Trans Am No! Please! Not this one! I mean it can go 160 mph man. Well, at least it *looks* as though it can. Actually it runs out of petrol before it gets to 45 mph. The fan belt is as long as the Daz lady's washing-line. And that funny Phoenix logo on the bonnet?

Bentley Turbo Known endearingly as the Bentley 'Turdo'. For a once famous company to build something as ugly as Engelbert is beyond reason.

Rolls-Royce (post 1970) They used to make nice cars.

Daf Very Luxembourg. Very EEC. Although I believe they're made in the Netherlands.

Austin Maxi Invariably driven by the Uncle Arthurs of this world who buy one car in a lifetime.

Mazda Mazda Spazda as we say in our country.

Triumph TR7 A blot on an otherwise perfect copybook. A lousy swan song to the company that produced some of the best.

Beach Buggy Help me Rhonda, rid me of this car. Those little sporty steering wheels, fat tyres and glass fibre chassis are very dated cool.

BMW 5 Series One suspects that a relative of Mr. Volvo had a hand in this one. No wonder they're being so heavily advertised these days.

CLASSIC COOL

Aston Martin DB 2, 3, 4, 5, 6 especially the drophead versions. (Avoid the DBSV8 and the Lagonda.)

Alfa Romeo Montreal. Spider. Lungo.

Alvis Any.

Austin Healey 3000 (Mks 1-3).

AC Cobra. 427 and 428.

Bentley 4½ litre. Mk 6, R and S1 Types.

BMW The early 3 Series. The later 6 Series.

Bristol Any.

Cadillac 1959 Eldorado. 1959 Eldorado Biarritz. 1959 Eldorado Brougham (made in Italy).

Citroën The Light 15 and Big 6 (the 'Maigret' Citroëns). The DS and DE (the General de Gaulle, Left Bank Citroëns). The 2CV (farmer, student, anti-hero chic).

Daimler 250 V8 Saloon (like the Jag Mk2s but with a Daimler engine). Dart. Sp250.

De Tomaso Pantera. Deauville.

Ferrari Any whatsoever. Even if they're not red. Especially, the Testarossa.

Fiat Dino (Very rare) Spyder or Coupé.

Ford GT40. V8 Pilot.

Iso Grifo.

Jensen CV8. Interceptor.

Jaguar D Type. E Type Mk1 – 3.8 litre. XK 120. XK 140. XK 150. Mk2 – 3.4 and 3.8 litre. S Type – 3.4 and 3.8 litre.

Lamborghini Miura.

Lotus Elan S1-S4 (The Emma Peel mobile). Lotus '7' ('The Prisoner' mobile). Elan Plus 2.

Mini/Austin Cooper and Cooper 'S'. These were the saloon cars that raced Brands Hatch in the Sixties.

Morgan 4/4 S.1. Plus 4. Plus 8.

Morris Minor. Minor Convertible. Traveller.

Mercedes-Benz Various. 190SL (1954-62). 300SL Gull Wing. 230SL (1963-67). (Avoid 250SL Sports.)

Maserati Mistrale. Ghibli. Indy. Bora. Khamsin.

Montiverdi 375/4.

MG MGA. (MGB, MGC, MGBGT, MGCGT are almost cool, but wait a few years.)

Peugeot 402B, 202U.

Porsche 911 all varieties – preferably without the little luggage rack on the back. (Thank you Citroën.)

Chevrolet Impala (1959) The one with the rear that looks like a fan dancer's tantrum.

Triumph All the TR models apart from the TR7 and the Stag.

V.W. Karmann Ghia. Beetle, any model. '250,000 miles and never failed a road test', 'buried in Libyan desert for five months, engine started first time', etc.

BIKER COOL

Fairly minimal unless the sun shines relentlessly, there's no law about crash helmets, and there's a close companion close behind.

Marianne Faithful was the girl on a motorcycle. Fonda and

Hopper were the final culmination of all those quickly dated Corman biker movies of the Sixties with stirring titles like *Angels from Hell*, *Hells Angels*, *Bikers from Hell*, *Hells Angels' Sex Party*, *Hells Angels' Tupperware Party*.

In the old wet grimy Metropolis, bikers dispatch and are dispatched with alarming regularity.

Old English bikes (Triumph, Norton, Matchless); Italian bikes (Ducati, Laverda, Moto Guzzi); German bikes (BMW); U.S. bikes (Harley Davidsons of every description, notably the 1200cc Electra Glide) are cool.

Jap bikes aren't. And since they comprise ninety-two per cent of the market, that's all that remains to be said on the subject.

THE BUS

It may not be fair, but anyone seen regularly on a bus after the age of twenty-eight may be considered a failure in life. End of chat.

THE TUBE

The Underground. The Subway. The Metro.

Despite the crush and the toilet-oriented smell, the rush-hours, drunks and lowlife, sufficient film directors have felt the underground to be an area of untapped cool. The concrete. The tubing. The haunting hissing sounds. Murkiness and electric oily danger – sufficient atmosphere to create an alternative concrete world with all the Stygian trimmings. *The Taking of Pelham 123. The French Connection. Subway. Diva. Death Wish. The Warriors. The District Line Crazies.*

All very well, all very cinema verité but at the end of the day whoever heard of a film director travelling by tube?

In any case, here are some underground rules. Mostly passive. Most of them don'ts.

Never run to catch a train Late for an interview? Too bad, see *Dole Cool* for further advice.

Stand Shoulders hunched. Hands in pockets. That well practised 'You're never alone with a Strand' look works well in this environment.

Look bored But don't eye contact with any one. Remember there's always a loony lurking somewhere just dying to talk to someone.

Do a difficult crossword (Times/Telegraph) Fill it in quickly, randomly and totally incorrectly just to get up the noses of the real crossword fillers.

Avoid a crush Sorry but you'll just have to wait for the next one. And the next one after that if necessary.

Avoid the falling passenger

There's always one who forgets to hold on to anything as the train alters its momentum.

Avoid playing walkmans too loudly Upset OAPs can, and will, stare you out.

Don't read another's paper Unless it's the *Sun* and you're desperate for a good laugh.

Don't eat fish and chips. McDonald's milkshakes or crisps.

Don't do any paper work of any kind How many times have you seen those goody-goody Clive Sinclair types frantically biroing all over their Company reports and computer printouts?

Don't smoke Some big bastard vigilante will ultimately call your bluff and then you'll blush and say you forgot the rules and the whole carriage will eat you for dinner. Maybe not today, maybe not tomorrow but someday. . .

Avoid the alien sex fiend But don't forget that to help out someone in distress is cool and in gratitude they may allow you to do later that which the 'fiend' had in mind.

THE TRAIN

More refined. More oldie worldie, but equally frustrating and often

slower. 'We apologise for the ninety minute delay between Clapham Junction and Waterloo, a bunch of nomadic Mesopotamian peasants inadvertently crossed a line during our teabreak.'

The romance of trains is rarely seen in reality.

The Orient Express. Vanishing Ladies. Murders. James Bond adventures. Corridors. Border checks. First-Class. Sleepers with Marilyn Monroe parties (see the film *Some Like it Hot*) with alcohol in hot water bottles, and travelling room-mates in baby-doll nighties, etc. All these have their place but it's strictly for the movies, and in the case of the M.M. scene strictly for fantasy. The only cool thing you can do on trains is to terminate trainspotters with extreme prejudice.

AIRLINES

Concorde wherever possible. Minimum flying time two hours fifteen minutes. Maximum – the haul to New Zealand. Destination – an international complex, a stop over and warm weather to greet you. Casual wear is fine. Tracksuits are definitely out. Plenty of hand luggage (travelling light) and essentials close to hand – Duracel batteries, novel, passport, money, peardrops, Browning automatic, amphetamines, hay fever tablets, cyanide pills – in fact anything that looks like the front cover of a pulp Sixties spy novel.

The Last Call Most important – the Cools always wait for the 'last call'. You know it's the last call because the female announcer says 'This is the last call'. Even after the last call has been announced, wait a little longer till they announce the 'final call'. And then with the odd drop of perspiration beginning to form, wait to see if they call your name personally. If they don't, run like shit for the relevant gateway. Whatever else, you've got to be last to board that plane. If you manage to hold up the aircraft while the hostess announces 'We're waiting for someone' to the other passengers, you've made it.

Getting comfortable Make sure you get an aisle seat. Preferably

non-smoking. Even if you smoke, you can always go for a stroll or go 'to the bathroom'.

Avoid the in-flight movie The pix are always out-of-sync with the sound, and the sound quality is usually so bad some old grannie is going to be asking you every three seconds 'Wad he say? Wad he say? – Tell me the whole plot from the beginning.'

Occasionally, it is satisfying to inform a friend that you've seen a hot movie that hasn't been shown back home yet – 'Yeah, I finally caught it on the way back from Jakarta.'

Avoid Music Channel 6 The AOR (Adult Orientated Rock) MOR (Middle of the Road) James Darren collection which, although labelled as rock music, is usually the reject B sides of Manilow and Denver.

Ignore the take-off safety procedure 'See that guy studying the take-off safety procedure, he's really keen. He's obviously never flown before.' Even if you haven't, and you are keen to observe, the chances are you're on a DC10 making its last flight before being sold off to the New Haiti People's Republic Airline. Basically it's always uncool to follow procedure. If the jet is going

to bounce no amount of toy oxygen masks and kiddicraft dinghies are gonna help you.

Don't read the in-flight magazine They're 'written by failed Geography 'O' level students for failed English Language 'O' level students.

Eat the in-flight food with disgust But eat it all . . . and the person's next to you if no-one's looking.

Order a special meal beforehand Eg vegetarian, kosher or steak and chips ('I'm allergic to everything else'). You will then be asked to make yourself known to the flight attendant which is fairly cool in itself.

Upgrade to First Class Sometimes being the last standby passenger on board will automatically grant you this privilege. You won't have to pay and you get as much champagne and Beluga as you want.

Don't talk to other passengers *Airplane 1* provides a reasonable guide of passengers to avoid. Alarm bells will be ringing if you spot two nuns, a priest, a couple on their second honeymoon and a diabetic nurse. Not to mention the drug addict. The hypochondriac. The alcoholic. The snorer. The kids on speed. The 'my boyfriend doesn't understand me anymore' type. These are all compulsive talkers just waiting to spill it out to anyone who looks as if they might speak their language. Either change seats immediately, pretending you've been waiting to be re-united with a friend. Or pretend to take a couple of sleeping tablets and when they're not looking slip them into the offending person's Jack Daniels.

The Emergency Landing Here you gotta be really cool. It's important to get to the back of the aircraft – since it's supposed to be safer. But don't show signs of panic, just walk with extreme gusto. When you're settled ask the stewardess calmly for a task. Hopefully she'll allocate you one of the back exit doors. If she does you're in with a chance, since you'll be out of the aircraft first. (Incidentally this is a good time for a last ditch attempt at the Mile High Club membership [see *Cool Sex*]).

Finally, if you come out unscathed – don't forget those passport stamps.

THOUGH single is best, occasionally two heads are better than one. Cool couples are an enigma. Do they add up or do they subtract? Certainly the strong will dominate the weak but what happens when it's the wrong one that succeeds? Was it inevitable that Lennon and McCartney should become overshadowed by Ono and Eastman? Are Harold Evans and Tina Brown really the golden match we are led to believe or would we rather see a more selfless arrangement on the lines of Bob Geldof and Paula Yates?

Obviously the trick is to grow stronger as a result of the union. The trick is also to maintain your independence. Ultimately if the couple is to be cool the result should be one where the whole world falls in love with you both. A weak link and it's back to being single again. Here are some of the signs to look for.

COOL COUPLE SIGNS

- You always leave your partner at the door of a party and meet up with him/her when you leave.
- You sometimes take separate holidays.
- You have totally separate careers.

- You have totally separate bank accounts.
- You don't kiss in public (but you can link arms).
- You both receive Oscars on the same night.
- He pays the mortgage on the town house, she pays it on the cottage. (N.B. Mr. doesn't mind being a house husband if Miz has a job that is better paid than his, because it enables him to get the novel written, compose songs, do the definitive video on Modern Fatherhood, etc.)
- You take the bullet that was meant for him and vice versa.
- One of you interrogates a suspect (Mr. Nasty) while the other (Mr. Nice) offers a cigarette.
- When one dies the other refuses to ever look at another man or woman (at least not for a couple of months anyway).

UNCOOL COUPLE SIGNS

Here are some of the signs to look for in an uncool couple. If you suspect any of the following bad habits are creeping in, terminate the relationship instantly.

- Unisex dressing. Especially matching jumpers and bath robes.
- You argue in front of friends when you're out over who's turn it is to drink and *not* drive.
- You start sentences with 'we think that' or 'we believe'.
- You stay in and turn down invitations because 'Little Mouse or Huggy Bear has got a cold and I ought to look after him/her'.
- You always get invited out as a couple, never separately.
- You fight in public.
- You cry in public.

■ You bore your friends with details of his/her infidelity and coldness to you of late.

■ You stick rigidly together at parties and show the world how much in love you are.

■ You hold hands.

■ You ask guests to leave dinner parties at 11.00 pm.

■ You yawn together.

■ You go to bed early.

COOL COUPLES

The Burtons (Liz and Dick).

Captain Furillo and Joyce Davenport (Hill Street Blues).

David Bailey/Jean Shrimpton (swinging Sixties couple).

David Bailey/Marie Helvin (swinging Seventies couple).

Terence Stamp/Jean Shrimpton (classic cool swinging Sixties couple).

Norman and Wenda Parkinson (aristocratic/jet-set photographer cool).

The Macbeths (Lord and Lady).

Spencer Tracy and Katharine Hepburn (all the superlatives of a cool couple on or off screen).

Bogart and Bacall (only in the movies, not in their private life).

Edward and Mrs. Simpson (his Kingdom for hers).

Jessica Lange and Sam Shepard (a current Hollywood favourite).

Cecil Beaton and Greta Garbo (he snapped, she snapped back).

Laurence Olivier and Vivien Leigh (he stayed sane, she didn't).

Bonnie and Clyde (he drove, she shot).

Charlotte Rampling and Jean Michel Jarre (he plays, she acts).

Dempsey and Makepeace (off-screen shenanigans).

Karl Lagerfeld and Inès de la Fressange (Coco & Co.)

Fred Astaire and Ginger Rogers (cool, suave, genius dance partners).

Angelica Huston and Jack Nicholson (he's nearly finished having a good time, she's very patient).

Nic Roeg and Teresa Russell (a star director and his star).

Ted Hughes and Sylvia Plath (passion, suicide. *Ariel* and *Crow*).

Mel Brooks and Anne Bancroft.

Eric Clapton and Patti Boyd.

Fergie's mum and the polo-playing Argentinian.

NOT SO COOL COUPLES

Sarah Keays and Cecil Parkinson (Publish and be damned; she did; he was).

Sean Penn and Madonna (she wants to be photographed, he beats up photographers).

Tatum O'Neil and MacEnroe (she wants to play Wimbledon, he wants to play Hollywood).

Brooke Shields and George Michael (she likes dolls, he likes Dolbys).

Joan Collins and Peter Holm.

Hart to Hart (he likes facelifts, she likes facelifts).

Jane Fonda and Tom Hayden.

Klaus Von Bulow and Andrea Reynolds (she's looking after him while his wife's asleep).

Aaron and Candy Spelling (the parents of Dynasty and Pam Ewing's son 'Kistopher').

Johnnie Hallyday and Sylvie (they parted years ago but no one told *Paris Match*).

Pia Zadora and Hubby (she wants

a career, he bought it for her).
Britt and Slim Jim (she's getting older, he's getting wiser).
Grace Jones and Dolf Lundgren (she beats him at arm wrestling, he lets her).

Farrah Fawcett and Ryan O'Neil.
Rod Stewart and Rod Stewart (an enduring love affair).
Jeffrey Archer and Jeffrey Archer (likewise).

THE CHICKS

- Marie and Jerry.
- Regan and Goneril.
- Celine and Julie.
- Bette Davis and Joan Crawford.
- Mandy Rice-Davis and Christine Keeler.

THE CHAPS

- Donald Sutherland and Elliot Gould.
- Woodward and Bernstein (The Watergate Reporters).
- Bowie and Jagger.
- Jagger and Richard (the Glimmer Twins).
- Lennon and McCartney.
- Butch and Sundance.
- Saatchi and Saatchi.
- Holmes and Watson.
- Peter Cooke and Dudley Moore.
- Errol Flynn and David Niven ('Cirrhosis by the Sea' – the home they shared in their Hollywood heyday).

THE CHUMPS

- George Michael/Andrew Ridgely (Wham/Splat).
- Ronnie and Reggie.
- Peter Fonda and Dennis Hopper.
- Charles and Sebastian.
- Starsky and Hutch.
- Greavsie and Saint.
- Little and Large.
- Cannon and Ball.
- Owen and Steele.

Dinner Parties

CHILLI. Stew. Beans on toast. Fish and chips. Faglioli with zamponi. Swordfish steaks. Sheep's testicles on rye.

It doesn't really matter what you give them so long as there's plenty of it, and it's washed down with plenty of cold champagne and averagely pricey plonk.

Lighting is by subtle lamplight and a thousand flickering candles. Warmth is provided by a glowing fire accompanied by the excellence of the conservation and company. Music is strictly background, some soft soothing Ella or Miles, or some Glenn or Bing if you're in the mood. The Nat King Cole can wait till after dinner.

When the Cools greet their guests, they do so in T-shirts and faded 501s. They then ply the assembled company with liberal amounts of Dry Martinis, Bloody Marys, Bellinis and champagne. Once the conversation has got into gear the host will then retire to shower and change into smart threads, return, change record, announce that dinner is about twenty minutes away and I think I'll have that Red Eye and tonic now.

Food is always served at the table, preferably in a dining room. White linen and foreign ashtrays are in abundance and every piece of matching cutlery, every glass is squeaky, sparkling clean. The food is served with a minimum of fuss, the cool host maximizing his or her time at the table with a dazzling array of guests, rather than flapping around in the kitchen.

Occasionally, a famous guest will be present. Occasionally, a little surreptitious match-making may be in evidence. Overall, the feeling is one of the 'beautiful and chosen' responding to the 'chosen and beautiful'.

The most crucial element is the selection of the dinner guests. The least crucial element is which way to pass the bloody port. Just get the Taylor's over here P.F.Q.

HOW TO MAXIMIZE SUCCESS

The Cools make it a rule that babies and young children are not allowed unless play-penned or doped up to the eyeballs. If a married couple has to leave early to relieve a babysitter they will incur punitive damage if it's before 4.00 am.

The Cool dinner party is anything but an 'After Eight' commercial dinner – no old uncle Ebenezers or witless Willies to bring the tone down. The gentlemen don't retire to the drawing room and the women are not left to discuss the finer qualities of Laura Ashley wallpaper or the size of Tom Selleck's wanger.

No holiday snaps. No drugs. No holiday, or wedding dirty videos. No vegetarian dishes. No 'No smoking' rule at dinner. And no joke sessions.

FORBIDDEN CONVERSATIONS

Avoid any people likely to be associated with, or likely to raise the following topics or conversational openings –

- Tony Hancock.
- Spitting Image.
- CAMRA.
- Hunt Supporters.
- South Africa.
- The PLO struggle.
- Unemployment.
- BBC v ITV.
- Decaffeinated coffee or polyunsaturated fats as a way to healthy living.
- Illness, especially colds and backpain – 'Oh, you're a doctor – well it just so happens I've got this mushy skin eruption in a very embarrassing place.'
- How much beer and curry you consumed last night.
- If I were dictator . . .
- The next election.
- Who was on the South Bank Show last Sunday.
- Who reads what newspapers?
- How, with the aid of this wonderful magazine on car mechanics that builds up week by week into a complete warehouse of irrelevance, I repaired my old Volvo Estate.

ENCOURAGE THE FOLLOWING TOPICS

- The meaning of life.
- Comparative earning powers.
- Sexual fantasies.
- The films of Erich Von Stroheim.

- 'What I'd do with a million pounds'.
- Computer bank-account fraud.
- The awful dress sense of a close acquaintance.
- The relative merits of New York vis a vis L.A. and vice versa.
- What a prat Andy Warhol was last time you saw him.
- The Bahamas during winter.
- Naughty things you did at school.
- How many different flavour vodkas you tried when you were last in Russia.

WHO TO INVITE

Amongst old school chums, anarchic reprobates, polar opposites, crazy colleagues, beautiful cousins, foreign correspondents, media stars, social climbers and a wild choice of friends of friends' best friends, it's best to have a good mix of different opinions, professions, physical looks and IQ levels.

Boy girl, boy girl boy girl is an option not a necessity. And despite the fact that you want everyone to get on, the cool host will occasionally throw in the odd experiment or two to keep it all good healthy fun. Like sitting a journalist next to an advertising copywriter (which one is telling the truth?), or a Greenpeace supporter next to the French chargé d'affaires.

In an ideal world, a guest list might be drawn from the following:

Anthony Burgess
Alan Whicker
David Attenborough
John Piper
Joanna Lumley
Selina Scott
Helen Mirren
Isabella Rossellini
Clive James
Alan Bennett
Edna O'Brien
David Puttnam
Greta Scacchi
Jack Nicholson
Brian Eno
Nicholas Roeg
Doris Lessing
Jean Muir
The Bishop of Durham
John Huston
Tina Turner
Daryl Hannah
Sigourney Weaver
Lawrence Durrell
Roman Polanski
Richard Ingrams
Tina Brown
Kate Bush.

In an imperfect world you may be saddled with the following:
Divine
Roger Moore
Bernard Manning
Klaus Von Bulow
Andy Warhol
Bernie Grant
Peter Langan
Margaret Trudeau
Yoko Ono
Alexei Sayle

Sir John Gielgud
Ivan Lendl
Madonna
Jackie Collins
Britt Ekland
Janet Street Porter
Colin Welland
Tony Curtis
Vidal Sassoon
Clive Sinclair
Samuel Beckett (brings his own knife and fork)
Oliver Reed (brings his own liver).

NIGHTCLUBBING

With the exception of the Grace Jones album, the Cools are very wary of the aforementioned pastime.

Whatever city, in whatever country they find themselves, Mr. and Miz are only interested in the strictly upmarket and totally exclusive. They know what's in and where to go. It's wherever they find themselves.

Dazzlingly dressed in dinner jackets and diamonds, the Cools travel in a floating party of six to eight people. If they feel like dancing it's with one of their own. They never dance with strangers. They find pick-ups and their concomitant conversation totally alien and in exceptionally bad taste.

Drinking only ice-cold champagne they dance economically and expertly. They leave in a timely flurry amid the following eyes of other late revellers, to catch cabs, Concordes and early morning breakfast in America.

UNCOOL NIGHT MOVES

Standing outside in ridiculous clothing waiting to be granted entrance to a club is beneath contempt, and it could be the uncoolest move you ever make.

Even if you're not subjected to such a humiliation there are plenty of ways you could slip up –
- Getting stuck in the toilet window, trying to gain entrance.
- Getting stuck in the toilet window of next door's takeaway, trying to gain entrance to a club.
- Dancing like John Travolta.
- Dancing around like Max Wall.
- Dancing around handbags.
- Dancing on your own, but pretending to be with the person dancing next to you who's dancing with someone else.
- Dancing to 'Jig-a-jig' by East of Eden.
- Chanting the words to songs, eg 'Hi Ho Silver Lining!' when the DJ turns the sound down.
- Entering dance competitions to the 'Birdy Song' (and winning).
- Snorting recently purchased, highly expensive baking-powder in the loo.
- Catching the bus home, pissed and penniless without so much as a phone number for your trouble.

ONE OF the most personal. One of the most obsessive. One that governs all the rest. Like accent, class and dress, music is a maker and a breaker. Whatever the music, like fashion, it is continually redefined and ever changing. Some music stands the test of time, some doesn't. Some of it simply can't make up its mind.

The Cools live their lives inside one endless soundtrack. One that changes to fit a multiplicity of chameleon-like moods. When the adrenalin flags music provides the vital shot.

It's Sunday morning, the party's over, the fair-haired stranger sleeps on. Music from the *Mood Tape* (a horn concerto, some Gregorian plain song or Peruvian pipe music) follows your silk-robed figure as you pad around the sun-filled apartment, trying to decide what to eat for breakfast and how the unfolding day will take shape.

The week goes by and suddenly it's Saturday evening again. The dormant tiger re-awakens and is carefully guided through a fevered electric cocktail of sounds known as the *Regeneration Tape* (Mott the Hoople: 'All the Way to Memphis', Billy Idol, George Thorogood and the Destroyers, Roxy Music: 'Do the Strand'). This one knows how to fill every room and forewarns neighbouring communities to lock up their daughters and take children under the age of

eighteen inside. 10-9-8 takes you through bathtime. 7-6-5 through the vital collection of threads. 4-3-2 through various perfumes, colognes, coiffeured styles and the first Turkish cigarette of the day. 1 – a quick once over in the mirror.

Zero – the *Cruising Tape* (The Stones: 'Gimme Shelter', Grace Jones: 'Bumper to Bumper', ZZ Top: 'Eliminator') takes over from central computer. 'The Midnight Rambler' guns 12 cylinders into action as the red receding bonnet is pointed in the direction of the uptown city lights.

Music covers everything. It's not just rock and roll. Classical is cool. Opera is cool. A small film soundtrack collection is a must. Jazz music of all types retains a liberal party following. Designer music (Eno, Andreas Vollenweider, George Winston and Philip Glass) is a dubious cross between relaxed and bored cool.

Concerts Concert going is no big deal. (Everyone's seen someone, somewhere). Past reminiscences are questionable cool, but if you ever saw Jimi Hendrix, the Stones with Brian or Mick Taylor, John Lennon, Bob Marley, then all that's left to be said is Bernstein, Brendel, and Brubeck.

Books/Magazines Forget rock and roll books, magazine articles and pop trivia. Most music journalists are failed pop stars.

Lyrics Knowing the words to a song is OK but remember lyrics date very quickly and you could sound very foolish crooning Marakesh Express in the company of your uptown friends.

The Guitar Better to know a little of some other instrument if all you can manage is 50 three-chord folk songs on the acoustic guitar. Playing guitar on the underground (busking) is highly uncool and doesn't even warrant *Dole Cool* status. Players who indulge in songs from *Cats* and themes from *The Deerhunter* should be hanged by their G-strings. Players who attempt 'Stairway to Heaven' or 'Angie' should die the death of a thousand plectrums.

The Piano Piano playing is highly cool. The more, the cooler. Even if you're not that good. It's highly recommended to learn the first ten bars of *Moonlight Sonata* or *Für Elise* perfectly. All you do then is stop, stand up, shut the piano and tell people you're not in the mood. You'll be reeling them in. The ability to play Boogie-Woogie, even badly so long as it's loud, your shirt sleeves rolled up and a filter tip cigarette hanging casually from your mouth, is equally cool (R.I.P. Ian Stewart).

Technology Beware of O.D'ing on technology. Every Cool's gonna have a compact disc player and a graphic equalizer one day so there's plenty of time. No one is more of a bore than the 'I'm a Hi Fi

250 RTZ low noise kilowatt' freak.

Car Stereo Buying a car stereo that outvalues your car by 250% is nothing to be proud of.

Pop Videos Pop videos, in most cases, are examples of extreme self-indulgence, disguised as art, Frankie Goes to Hollywood being a prime example. Odd exceptions include Michael Jackson's *Thriller*, Bowie's *China Girl*, Dire Straits' *Making Movies*, *Take on Me* by A-Ha and *My Way* by Sid Vicious. Video cafes and pubs are where Kevin and Sharon simply dream about being cool. As background music MTV will suffice in your West Coast Hotel.

Records Record collections continue to be a crucial source of cool credibility.

Original labels, original mono-recordings, imports, obscure track listings and deletions all add up. Buying Neil Young's 'Decade' triple album for three unreleased tracks is mere folly since you could've spent the same money on improving the vital gaps in your early John Coltrane or Charlie Parker section. Bootlegs, once essential, are dated cool.

Since home taping can take care of virtually everything and money doesn't grow on trees, check your score on the following –

FIFTY ESSENTIAL ALBUMS FOR A RECORD COLLECTION

1 Astral Weeks (1968) Van Morrison
A once in a lifetime composition. Enough imagery and musical styles to filla dozen albums, it has all the artistic grace of eight Van Goghs set to music. (NB, every Cool knows that the reeds were only added at the last minute.)

2 In a Silent Way (1969) Miles Davis
11 am Sunday morning in a Manhattan Penthouse. You prepare tea while your overnight guest showers. You've never heard a trumpet like it; its pedigree is as long as an Abel Gance movie.

3 The Koln Concert (1975) Keith Jarrett
Solo Steinway takes four strolls around your soul, treble cleaving it and then putting it back together again.

4 For Your Pleasure (1973) Roxy Music
Deviant S&M wet London nite life set to music. A pleasant reminder that the Seventies weren't all bad.

5 Undercurrent (1962) Bill Evans
The greatest album cover ever. Who cares about the rest of the record.

You never know, it might even be good.

6   Revolver (1966) The Beatles
Stuck squarely between adolescence and adulthood, this is when the kissing stopped and the drugs began to take hold. Twenty years on it still wipes the floor with the best of them.

7   Electric Ladyland (1968) Jimi Hendrix
Jimi as Dr. Who firmly at the controls of the Tardis. Perhaps he'll return one day.

8   The Dream of Blue Turtles (1985) Sting
Recorded with some of the snazziest young talent of the New York jazz scene. A now familiar lofty voice rises above a mixture of musical styles and rhythms to discuss current issues of the day. One world, world peace, megapower, sanity, etc.

9   Parallel Lines (1978) Blondie
More pure power pop than Macca ever produced in a lifetime.

10   Marquee Moon (1977) Television
Strangely strange but oddly normal TV (Tom Verlaine) programme.

11   New Gold Dream (1982) Simple Minds
London to Los Angeles. Subliminal music conjures up shining highways and squeaky clean sanitised hotel rooms. Modern music for modern times.

12   Exile on Main Street (1972) Rolling Stones
Two hours of uninterrupted Jack Daniels, joints, hookers, busted TV sets, junk food and pills. The best party of the Seventies. Yet strangely I remember very little of it. Best phone Keith up and ask him.

13   This Year's Model (1978) Elvis Costello
Chelsea boys and girls trash it up and down the Kings Road. All they needed was a sniff of love and understanding.

14   Layla (1970) Derek and The Dominos
Electric blues and rock set to music to produce the finest non-psychedelic session to come out of a syringe.

15   Piper at the Gates of Dawn (1967) Pink Floyd
Alice in Wonderland meets Pooh Bear in the toy cupboard, while outside the wind blows in the willows. Syd Barrett at his eccentric best.

16   Born to Run (1975) Bruce Springsteen
It was and still does.

17   The Original Soundtrack (1975) 10 C.C.
Clever punks indeed. Full of style and polish signifying everything.

18   Colosseum Live (1971) Colosseum
The best live record alive, despite being recorded in a Victoria Station toilet.

19   Rain Dogs (1985) Tom Waits
Twenty-one tracks of witty, edgy and angular urban blues, polkas, wet-back tangos and demented, merry-go-round instrumentals. From the man who once said he slept through the Sixties, this album like all his previous gems continues to chronicle a less well known side of American culture.

20   Before and After Science (1977) Brian Eno
Ambient music recorded by computer. Very popular amongst HALs, MOTHERs and NEXUS 6s.

21 Can't buy a Thrill (1972) Steely Dan
Who needs to tour when you've got a studio? Musicians' musicians' musicians make musicians' music.

22 Five Leaves Left (1969) Nick Drake
Sleepy English country village amid everlasting English summer witnesses haunting end (suicide?) to talented and cult English songwriter. Ideal for 4.00 am instrospections.

23 Unknown Pleasures (1978) Joy Division
Sparse, statuesque, monolithic. Like a vast desolate landscape. This their first of two, before evolving into New Order, features the talented Ian Curtis before he committed suicide. Musically original. Emotionally harrowing.

24 Pet Sounds (1966)

25 Surf's Up (1971)

26 Holland (1973)
Three milestones in the history of a one man (Brian Wilson) music industry which created the California saga – **The Beach Boys**.

27 '77 (1977) Talking Heads
Everyone's got 'Little Creatures', but have you got their first? Catchy, indefinable pop music from a totally original combo not renowned for catchy indefinable music. Quite in-

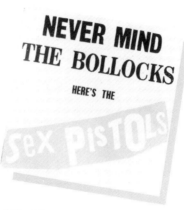

definable.

28 Never Mind the Bollocks (1977) Sex Pistols
Dirty, foulmouthed degenerates, destroy the last remnants of the Glittersaurus and return music back whence it came.

29 6 & 12 String Guitar (1972) Leo Kottke
The acoustic Hendrix let loose on folk and blues. The album that makes you do to your Yamahas what Townsend did to his Gibson SGs.

30 Kate Bush (1985) Love of Hounds
The wind, wuthering heights, Cornish coasts, Heathcliffs, wild hills and deals with God. Atmospheric feminine intuition of the highest order.

31 Court and Spark (1974) Joni Mitchell
Despite walking the hippy tightrope for many years, Mitchell's masterpiece is moody poetry set to magnificent music.

32 Rattus Norvegicus (1977) The Stranglers
Fun, heavy and hard. Misogynistic rockers producing some excellent tongue-in-cheek tunes, that sound like a cross between The Doors and The Pistols.

33 Blonde on Blonde (1966),

34 Blood on the Tracks (1974) Bob Dylan may not be the ideal dinner guest. He may have bored you with 'Born Again' albums, but these milestones can not be ignored from a former cool master (retired). A retrospective is sure to be on the way.

35 Imagine (1971) John Lennon
Simple songs. Simple tunes. A total understanding of the musical media. A fine mixture of idealism and absolute bitchiness.

36 On the Beach (1974) Neil Young
Canadian hitchhiker falls for bright west coast lights. Becomes disillusioned. But stays on for a while to take the piss.

37 Heroes (1977) David Bowie
Berlin. V2s Nukoln. A touch of the old Aryans on this one but he falls the right side of the wall.

38 Transformer (1972) Lou Reed

High camp New York pop tunes with delicious harmonies and lyrics. Experience disguised as innocence.

39 Dire Straits (1978) Dire Straits

From New Orleans to Watford, this tight economic package of dreamlike guitar playing takes a lot of beating.

40 Bop Till You Drop (1979) Ry Cooder

Funky whiteman honky come struttin' around here with his blue Strat, pink suit and polka-dot tie. Funny, lively, sad, moody songs from the finest most innovative guitarist around.

41 Silk Degrees (1976) Boz Skaggs

The best nightclub/disco record for those who arrived late from dining out and were content to shuffle around in their tuxes and haute couture finery.

42 I Sing the Body Electric (1972) Weather Report

Weather Report deserve a lot of investigation. Here's a good place to start.

43 There's a Riot Goin' On (1971) Sly and the Family Stone

Super Sly, a Fallen Angel of *cool*, produced the best in bad-assed, super soul funky rhythms. Like 'Fresh' a mean mother of an album. Where are they now?

44 Strange Days (1968) Doors

Strange days indeed. Every collection should house some Doors. Either this or '13' or 'Weird Scenes Inside the Goldmine'.

45 Boys and Girls (1985) Bryan Ferry

Cool sophisticated Bri briefly escapes from his lyrics to concentrate on producing a series of atmospheric, rhythmic songs with some of the best names in the business. If you've got 'Another Time, Another Place' (1974), that counts too.

46 Supremes Greatest Hits (1976) Supremes

Indispensable collection of pop love songs sung by the First Lady of Soul.

47 Shades (1981) J.J. Cale

The King of Laid Back. Nay the Emperor. Virtually any of his will do. It's 2.00 am and you're having a meaning-of-life conversation while guzzling bootleg whisky. Why play three chords when you can play two?

48 Soul Mining (1983) Matt [The The] Johnson

Brings that Uncertain Smile to the lips. Will we all be waiting for his next album the rest of our lives?

49 Arc of a Diver (1980) Steve Winwood

The man plays all the instruments. The man can sing. The man has been making sweet music since he was the teenage frontman with the Spencer Davis Group.

50 Django Reinhardt (Vogue Jazz Double 1976) Django Reinhardt

The gypsy with lightning fingers. With guest appearances by cool fiddler Stephane Grappelli. Reinhardt was a great influence on many a guitarist – McLaughlin, Clapton, Beck, to name but a few.

C O O L

Come Up and See Me (make me smile) Cockney Rebel
I Can't Get No (satisfaction) Rolling Stones
You Really Got Me The Kinks
Love is the Drug Roxy Music
Virginia Plane Roxy Music
Sorrow David Bowie
China Girl David Bowie
The American Simple Minds
The Sun Ain't Gonna Shine Any More The Walker Brothers
Complete Control The Clash
Games Without Frontiers Peter Gabriel
Shock the Monkey Peter Gabriel
See Emily Play Pink Floyd
All Along the Watchtower Jimi Hendrix
Need Your Love So Bad Fleetwood Mac
Albatross Fleetwood Mac
Anarchy in the UK Sex Pistols
Pretty Vacant Sex Pistols
Friday on My Mind The Easybeats
Don't Walk Away Renée The Four Tops
We Gotta Get Out of This Place The Animals
What a Fool Believes The Doobie Brothers
I Heard it Through the Grapevine Marvin Gaye
Dock of the Bay Otis Redding
Tears of a Clown Smokey Robinson
Every Breath You Take Police
When I Fall in Love Nat King Cole
Eleanor Rigby The Beatles

Hey Jude The Beatles
Strangers in The Night Frank Sinatra
Badge Cream
Running Up That Hill Kate Bush
A Forest The Cure
Bette Davis Eyes Kim Carnes
My Best Friend's Girl The Cars
Heart Full of Soul Yardbirds
In a Broken Dream Python Lee Jackson
You Can't Hurry Love The Supremes
Eloise Barry Ryan
The Letter The Box Tops
You're So Vain Carly Simon
Take A Walk on The Wild Side Lou Reed
No More Heroes The Stranglers
Holiday in Cambodia The Dead Kennedys
California Uber Alles The Dead Kennedys
Psychokiller Talking Heads
Because The Night Patti Smith
I'm On Fire Bruce Springsteen
Gimme Some Lovin' Traffic
X-Offender Blondie
Heart of Glass Blondie
Sultans of Swing Dire Straits
Another Girl, Another Planet The Only Ones
In a Rut The Ruts
Watching the Wheels John Lennon
Wild Thing The Troggs
Whisky in the Jar Thin Lizzy
Positively 4th Street Bob Dylan
I Only Want To Be With You Dusty Springfield
Atmosphere Joy Division
Rubber Bullets 10 C.C

I Got You Babe Sonny and Cher
You've Lost That Lovin' Feeling The Righteous Brothers
Dance Hall Days Wang Chung
My Way Sid Vicious

Godfather Parts 1 & 2 – Haunting Sicilian peasant music
Assault on Precinct 13 – John Carpenter's menacing electronic suspenser
Southern Comfort – Not available yet except by taping the video – Ry Cooder accoustic Swamp music plus some great Cajun tunes
Blade Runner – not the existing orchestra version but the original Vangelis score. Once again only available by taping the video
Midnight Express – Electronic sounds from Giorgio Moroder
2001 – As Zarathustra said. BOM BOM BOM BOM
Paris, Texas – Ry Cooder deep in the heart of Texas
Edge of Darkness – Eric Clapton and Michael Kamen
A Clockwork Orange – Electronic Beethoven that works
Repo Man – Various artists: Iggy Pop, Black Flag. U.S. hardcore comes of age
Diva – For the aria 'La Wally'
Picnic at Hanging Rock – For the atmosphere

COOL

CLASSICAL COOL

Elgar – The Enigma Variations and Cello Concerto

Sibelius – Symphony no. 5 and Finlandia

Mahler's 9 Symphonies particularly the 4th and 9th

Beethoven's 9 Symphonies particularly the 7th

Carl Orff – Carmina Burana (the aftershave music)

Mozart – more or less anything. Especially his piano concertos

Bach – Brandenburg Concertos and Klavier Temperiete

Pachelbel's Canon in D (the wool music)

Beethoven's last Sonatas

Liszt – Mephisto Waltz

Brahms – Violin Concerto

Saint-Saens – 3rd Symphony with Organ

Tchaikovsky – Piano Concerto no. 1, and the 6th Symphony

Rachmaninov – Piano Concerto no. 2

Schubert – 'B' flat Sonata opus posthumous

Mendelssohn – Cello Sonata

Dvorak – Cello Concerto

Ravel – Piano Concerto for the left hand

Handel's Messiah

Bruckner – Selected symphonies

OPERA COOL

An appreciation of opera is cool, but that doesn't mean to say all opera is necessarily good, as George Bernard Shaw once pointed out when talking of Wagner: 'Wagner has some great moments but some very long quarters of an hour', or Mozart's observation when comparing musical notes with a fellow composer: 'I liked your opera. I will now set it to music'.

Johann Strauss
Die Fledermaus

Richard Strauss
Der Rosenkavalier

Delibes
Lakme (British Airways music)

Bizet
Carmen
The Pearl Fishers

Verdi
La Forza del Destino
Requiem
Falstaff
Rigoletto
La Traviata

Puccini
Turandot
La Bohème

Wagner
Various including the Meistersingers, Tristan and Isolde, Tannhäuser and the Ring Cycle

Mozart
Cosi Fan Tutte
The Magic Flute
The Marriage of Figaro
Don Giovanni
Clemenza di Tito

Monteverdi
The Coronation of Poppaea

Benjamin Britten
Peter Grimes

UNCOOL MUSIC

Since music is a wide subject, the field is obviously very open to disastrous lapses of taste. So long as you realise you've been a naughty boy and make the requisite amends you are forgiven. But just in case. . .

Have you ever changed tapes at a party with your favourite New Order collection and ended up dancing to it on your own? Have you ever been guilty of sharing the delights of your ghetto-blaster with the rest of the world's sunworshippers on a crowded beach? (Perhaps it was Twisted Sister's loudest hits emanating from your Fiat Lada on Brighton Esplanade?)

Do you know what *acid rock* is? Do you mime a mean cardboard guitar to *No Sleep Till Hammersmith*? Have you ever tried to convert your closest friends to the dubious delights of Steve Hillage and Gong? Were you one of the audience who applauded Ravi Shankar's sitar playing at Bangladesh only to be informed that the man was, in fact, still tuning up?

Negative on all counts? Well this one might get you. Have you ever pointed out the good guitar bits on a record saying something like 'Quiet. Quiet. This is it. Listen to this bit. No, no, no. The next bit . . . no this bit . . . no this bit, etc., etc.'.

Still negative? OK – How many times have you seen Status Quo? How many free Hyde Park gigs did you go to during the Sixties? Have you ever applied for tickets to *Top of the Pops*, or written in for a radio request for someone in the forces?

If you're not guilty of any of the aforementioned, you're almost

there. There's just the record test to pass. Those forgotten embarrassments in your record collection that you can't quite force yourself to throw out. Those slender shrines that you maintain to ageing hippy crooners because they were the ones that were once beloved of the class of 1972.

Apart from the more obvious faux pas – Rolf Harris, Anita Harris, Max Bygraves, James Last, Tiny Tim, Val Doonican and John Denver – if you're still sheltering any of the following waxings best leave them on a market stall one Sunday, and quickly make good your escape when the coast is clear.

Frampton Comes Alive Well somebody must have a copy since it topped the charts both sides of the Atlantic for a few months.

Black Sabbath 'Paranoid', I bet you are.

Uriah Heap Very 'umble, very dated, not arf.

Grand Funk Railroad Very loud, very uncomfortable. An earlier incarnation of Sigue Sigue Sputnik.

Paul Anka 'Here's a song I wrote for a friend of mine' (ie because I can't sing).

Richard Clayderman The talented young pianist from France.

Johnnie Hallyday The extremely untalented rocker from France.

Mirielle Mathie The talented, but extremely boring chanteuse.

Plastique Bertrand Ze punk with talent (none of the others had!).

Glitter Pop Gary, Sweet, Boney 'M', Marmalade, Osmonds, David Cassidy, etc. Tie a yellow ribbon till blue in the face.

4-Skins Strength through Oi (ie 'oi got no brine').

Singer Songwriters Crosby & Nash, Crosby & Stills, Crosby & Young, Crosby & Coke. All those James Taylors. Melanie, etc.

Hippy Die Hards Gillan, Hawkwind, Saxon, Motorhead, Marillion, AC/DC, Scorpion.

Fag-Pop Aerosmith, New York Dolls, Kiss.

'Ride-On' Pop Barry White, Isaac Hayes.

Football Rock 'Good old Arsenal', 'Ossie had too much to dream last night and couldn't stop blowing bubbles'.

Tartan Rock Early Rod Stewart, Bay City Rollers Mk 1, 2 and 3.

Vegas Rock Old Darby and Joan farts like Eng., Tom Jones, Tony Bennett, Jack Jones. The exception being Frank Sinatra.

Short-arsed-foreign-crooner-rock Charles Aznovoice, Julio Iglesias, Neil Sedaka.

Rak pop Suzi Quatro, Mud, Hot Chocolate, Showaddywaddy, Mickie Most, Mickie Least.

Hersham Boys Sham 69. Down the pub. Down the club. Down the nick.

Xmas Records You can hear Slade laughing all the way to their Swiss bank.

Blind re-release pop Jose Feliciano still attempting to light his fire.

Funny Records Barron Knights, Ivor Biggun, Hilda Baker and Arthur Mullard, Ernie Wise accompanied by Emerson, Lake & Palmer. 'Ernie the Fastest Milkman in the West'.

'We've-produced-26-double-albums-rock' Chicago, Allman Brothers, Frank Zappa, etc.

Viva Espana pop He eased the safety catch off his Magnum 44, the most powerful handgun in the west. The greasy DJ was already lifting the stylus as he took aim. . .'

'No War – No Illness – No Poverty Pop' Yes. Boy George. Bronski Beat.

Dying to be Cool

'When it comes, it must be met beautifully and finely.'
(BETTE DAVIS – *Dark Victory*)
'Death's at the bottom of everything Martins, leave death to the professionals.'
(ORSON WELLES – *The Third Man*)

A LITTLE morbid perhaps but much of cool's substance is derived from its dark shadow. There are two attitudes to it. The first is reflected in the Bette Davis quote and is practised by those who see death as the ultimate cool gesture. The latter attitude is slightly more positive: it's for cool survivors. A cool death is admirable but you don't have to practise what you preach. Mostly the Cools prefer to be at the Clint Eastwood end of the trigger. You can know too much, too soon.

Cool deaths cover four basic areas –

The Sacrifice ie sacrificing your life for someone or something you believe in.

These are the religious and political martyrs. Everyone with 'Saint' in front of their name. Idealists who die for their beliefs and are either branded 'traitor' or 'patriot' depending on which side wrote the history books.

Cool sacrifices are best buddies dying for best buddies, ie those who took the slug for someone else, so long as it wasn't a case of being accidentally in the way.

Other sacrifices bring to mind all those ordinary GI's who dived on the grenade that landed near 'C' troop because they would've got it anyway. Plus all those who went on Rambo-style suicide missions but without any of the sophisticated hardware Sly had.

We recall interrogations where Mr. Cool chews the cyanide pill so he won't rat on his buddies or his country. 'Pain? I laugh at it!' he scoffs with contempt.

The Brave Death Doing it beautifully and finely since that bullet on closer observation has actually got your name on it.

Plenty in this category. Partially the result of a misguided Japanese philosophy that a brave death was the most important thing in life and includes The Samurai Cult. The kamikazes. The Knights of Bushido, etc.

On a less glamorous note, there are the firing-squadders of the Gary Gilmore type who go out with a defiant *'let's do it'* and who don't need a blindfold – just a last Chesterfield.

And let's not forget the Jimmy Cagney type from *Angels with Dirty Faces*. You know the scene. Father Pat asks him to turn yellow just before he gets the chair, so the street gang who worship him won't have a hero to look up to and will grow up to be good citizens. Jimmy, who's got enough on his mind already, naturally turns the jaundice for the good Fadder. The boys lose a hero but the heavenly chorus confirms that Jimmy's turned good guy.

Young Death *The light that shines twice as bright burns half as long, and you have burned so very brightly'.*

(TYRELL to his creation Roy – RUTGER HAUER in *Blade Runner*)

To ensure a place among the cool immortals, all you have to do is quit while you're ahead of the game.

Marilyn Monroe
Jimi Hendrix
Billy Holiday
James Dean
Sid Vicious
Edie Sedgewick
Buddy Holly
Brian Jones
Alain Fournier
Eddy Cochrane
John Lennon
Bob Marley
To name but a few.

Cheating Death Probably the most popular of the four. Players in this category get all the credit for almost dying but get to live as well.

Dangerous professions are somewhere in this one. Greenpeace. Bomb Disposal. War Photographers, eg Tim Page and Don McCullin. Being Bernard Manning's minder.

There's the odd survivor of three turns at the electric chair.

There's the odd WW2 pilot who bailed out without a parachute and lived to tell the tale. Eg Sergeant Nicholas Alkemade who bailed out of his Lancaster bomber at 18,000 ft without a parachute and lived. He woke up in thick snow and saw about him the trees that had broken his fall.

And finally, remember all the people who faked their death to collect on the insurance or to live a fresh life with a new identity (eg Reggie Perrin).

UNCOOL DEATHS

Nothing is more embarrassing than one of these –

■ Chasing bankrobbers who are heavily armed when you're not.
■ Dying 'on the job' or doing a 'Bruce Lee', ie having a heart attack while performing sex.
■ Committing suicide as a result of a suicide pact when your partner suddenly decides to change his/her mind.
■ The total excess way – John Belushi. Jimi Hendrix. Various participants in the film *La Grand Bouffe* who gastronomically gorge themselves to death.
■ Being shot while in bed with someone else's husband or wife (or both).
■ While on the bog. Sitting or standing, it doesn't matter.

■ Being run over by a Reliant three-wheeler.
■ Being run over by a bus.
■ Leaning casually against a wall at a party trying to impress someone, only to discover that what you're actually leaning against is an open window fourteen floors up.

WHEN THE EXCEPTION IS MURDER

Cool murders are revenge murders, crimes passionels and mercy killings. Few exist and to be cool the punishment must be made to fit the crime. For background material read Agatha Christie's *Ten Little Niggers* and catch a few Claude Chabrol films.

COOL SEX

COOL SEX is essentially sex without bodies. It's physical, but a physical presence rather than the old in and out.

What the Cools invest in is a slow physical build-up (he stared at her meaningfully for four hours across a crowded room) rather than the momentary end away product (Wham! Bam! Thank you Maam!). With the odd exception (see below) there's nothing intrinsically cool about the humping, pounding, groaning earth-moving experience that is the sex act. It involves too much effort, too much wanton want, too much ridiculous verbal interchange: 'Was it good for you? Was it good for you and you? How about you, you and you? Anyone want to know if it was good for me?' Above all it involves too much loss of self control.

If they're in the mood, the Cools can actually trigger off multiple orgasms at will, fully clothed, from four blocks away.

The naked body is vulnerable and whatever else the Cools are, they're never that.

James Dean wasn't interested in it. Randolph Scott, John Wayne, Robert Redford and Clint rarely did it in the movies.

Even in those films, 'the exceptions' below, where sex is the main event, notice how the clothes tend to remain on:

William Hurt and Kathleen Turner in *Body Heat*. An electric scene occurs after she has been relentlessly leading him on. He finally cracks and not before time. The result? A garden table is thrown through the French windows to gain entry to her house. Once in, he takes Kath there and then at the bottom of the stairs. (As far as we can tell much of her underwear

remains firmly on, and very nice it is too! – Barry Normanspeak.)

Marlon Brando and Maria Schneider in *Last Tango in Paris*. They meet as strangers in a vacant apartment. Not a word is spoken for the twenty minutes or so they engage in all manner of limb manoeuvres. (You see plenty of her body but very little of his. Thank you Mr. Bertollucci for small mercies.)

Jack Nicholson doing it with Jessica Lange on the kitchen table in *The Postman Always Rings Twice*. They can't stand each other at first but when the animal desire takes over, tough luck on the baking trays and the tea cakes. (Clothes remain firmly on, after all Jessica's a serious actress. Jack? He don't care either way.) ☛

The opening sequence in *Performance*. Chas (James Fox) and his night club hostess are engaged in a bit of the old S & M yet it's all filmed in the best possible taste. (Like putting credits over the naughty bits and intercutting the scenes of a nice car driving along nice roads in the nice countryside.)

Steve McQueen and Faye Dunaway in the *Thomas Crown Affair*. The famous chess game. The suggestive finger and eye movements. After a long stale-mate, McQueen says 'Let's play something else.' A

twenty minute snog ensues as they twirl ecstatically around the room. Cut to them in the sack. She's dying to do it again, but he's content to smoke Marlboro and read the Wall Street Journal.

Mickey Rourke and Kim Bassinger in *9½ Weeks*. A series of mildly kinky romps as commercials director Adrian Lyne indulges in a high-budget cinematic *Rude Food*. She is forced to wear a blindfold on their first date, and grovel for money on their last, while another time he feeds her the contents of a fridge. The real stars, however, are Rourke's Comme des Garçons clothing and his matt-black sin-bin. Probably the most erotic moment is the smooth automated flipping action of his Nakamichi cassette deck.

We conclude that for the Cools, the build up is the most important part. The aftermath is cool too – it's not enough to hand your partner one half of two lighted cigarettes as you face the ceiling in a post-coital extinct volcanic state. You must indulge in a little cool afterplay.

It's when you're expected to let out a secret or two.

Such as how when you were a child you escaped from the Bolsheviks with no possessions except a few family heirlooms. Or how you harbour secretly deep-seated fear of white rabbits, white bread and white mice.

COOL

Recollections and admissions like these, after sex, are one of the few times when the Cools open up to each other. This is usually done in a sad rather wistful 'isn't life strange' manner but never lasts long. Eventually the secret inner revelations of the cool soul are curtailed to keep others guessing. A long sigh will precede a deep and meaningful remark to bring conversation back to normal.

Eg *'Oh well, past is past.'* Or *'How about some beans on toast and a little Kir to wash it down with?'* Or *'Isn't there a Bunuel movie on the other channel?'* Or *'Could we try number 73 again, I think I'm getting another strange feeling?'*, etc., etc.

For the Cools, sex is essentially before and after. Not in-between. Every Cool is either an amazing sack artist or they don't bother at all.

GETTING WHAT YOU WANT WHEN YOU WANT IT

For Mr. Cool, there's always the Fonz approach. Direct. Unquestionable, instant. A snap of the fingers and she's there. This one shouldn't be overplayed too much however, after all snapping fingers can be a very tiring business. As an alternative Mr. Cool frequently favours the Cary Grant approach, ie she does all the work while he gets all the best lines.

Miz Cool doesn't even have to try that hard. She sees what she wants and within seconds she and the object of her desire are winging their way back to her hilltop apartment. Next morning two strong men in white coats come to take one gibbering exhausted wreck away to a health farm for a couple of weeks of complete rest and recuperation.

In the case of the Cool Couple, the build up is longer and more aggressive. There's more strategic planning, more chess games, more gifts, more wining and dining and nights at the opera. After some time has passed she asks: 'Have we been to bed yet?' He replies: 'I don't know, I can't remember.' They say: 'Let's do it now just in case we haven't.'

Occasionally you can wait cooly and patiently for what you want, while the fools rush in. Alan Bates got Julie Christie and the best end lines this way in *Far From the Madding Crowd*. This is still classed as questionable cool, however, and should not be encouraged. The Cools are first, last and always.

In personal relationships, the Cools know exactly how to handle themselves, especially at the outset of a relationship.

DON'T BE BLACKMAILED

The golden one. You can live a perfectly cool existence and then blow it all by losing your head to some little upstart because they happen to be a great sack artist. Definitely the downward path. If you're in danger of this happening spend a few minutes with *Health and Efficiency/Playgirl* and a bucket of ice cubes before you meet them. If this doesn't work get your mother/lawyer/analyst to phone you at the crucial moment. Under no circumstances should you 'put out' at someone else's command.

Keep your tongue in your mouth at all times
A tongue flopping all over your chest is a dead giveaway. It's OK to do it when you're eating, so long as the soup de jour doesn't dribble down your chin. Don't stare too much either. Too much Peter Lorre or Suè Ellen can ruin anyone's evening.

Don't make physical contact on the first three dates

When Kelly says 'do you want to come up for a nightcap?' we all know what she means. This is a difficult one, but imagine what will happen come the fourth date – she'll have spent a king's ransom on Janet Reger. 'If this stuff doesn't make him crack I don't know what will.'

Arrange plenty of early morning appointments to avoid staying the night at someone else's place

The Cools always prefer to play on home turf. They like to have complete control over the situation. If the other person won't play ball and expects you to stay with them, say you'd love to but the French are arriving early at your home for breakfast to discuss the Channel Tunnel and you still have to buy the croissants. Don't, whatever you do, use the old 'I've-got-to-get-up-early-to-do-my-paper-round' excuse.

Getting what you want *where* you want it

Cools who insist on knowing if they score higher doing it here rather than there, ie in a plane loo or under the bacon-counter at Harrods, are on questionable cool ground. If the curious allow us to proceed afterwards, the answer is generally held to be yes, some places are cooler than others, on the other hand it's very uncool to

tell anyone about it. The Cools don't need to advertise. Everyone knows they do it when and where they feel like it. If it happens to be at tea-time at the Ritz, tough on the tourists. Let them eat cake. Indeed one of the coolest occasions of public sex concerned the couple who made love in the middle of the tableau vivant of 'The Death of Nelson' in Madame Tussaud's with all the cannons going off.

COOL COUPLINGS

In the lift of a posh hotel

Either a quickie while the lift operator has his back turned, or a slow one with the lift stuck between the second and third floor.

At Christie's during an auction

Most people will be too involved in the bidding to notice although you may pick up one or two lots you hadn't bargained for if your arms are prone to flailing about.

In the Reading Room of the British Museum

Fine if you're both the silent types. If not, not.

On the beach at Bali-by-Sea

As the moon makes love to the waves. Don't forget to take your trunks off though.

On a city rushhour tube

Highly exciting after a stressful day

at the office. It's quite likely no one will notice or at least will *pretend* not to notice.

On Concorde

No ordinary flight this one. With only two hours to New York, you haven't exactly got much time.

At the Tate Gallery

'But Jasmin, Darling, this performing exhibit isn't even mentioned in the catalogue. Could it be one of those mobiles I've heard about?'

On *Question Time*

'Yes a question for the Member for Carshalton West. No, no . . . profuse apologies. I made a mistake.'

In a Ferrari 308 GTS while travelling down the M1

Exciting stuff. 'One second we were

going 70 mph . . . the next 20 mph . . . then 160 mph . . . then the engine blew up.'

In the bedroom

Highly original and quite unexpected.

UNCOOL COUPLINGS

In a launderette

You may be washing your 501s at the same time as her, but it's very tacky all the same.

In a cinema

Unless that's you up on the screen with Sigourney or Mel forget it.

In a BR train

Think of all those who have already had the same idea in the same compartment.

At Stringfellows

No one would notice because they're usually all at it themselves. Either that, or people will think it's just another in a long line of disco competitions.

At a Harrods Sale

Once again, no one would notice, and you'll probably end up being bought as an objet d'art by some fat loaded tourist.

On *Blind Date*

Funny yes – cool no. Worth it to see the look on Cilla's face though.

'Peter. You turned down lovely Maxine from Skegness and Tracy from Hull but you seem to be having a lorra fun with Sandra from Mayfair.'

UNCOOL SEX

'Je T'aime . . . Moi Non Plus' by Jane Birkin and Serge Gainsbourg
Groupies.
Emmanuelle films.
Confessions of films, eg a Bus Driver, a Shepherd, a Mortuary worker, etc.
Androgynous Boy George/Marilyn tea enthusiasts.
Jacuzzis.
Playboy culture.
Page 3.
Benny Hill.
George and Lynne.
Paul Raymond.
Tit and bum magazines.
Strippers with a heart of gold.
Bo.
Frankie Goes to Hollywood.
Kama Sutra cartoons.
Hollywood Wives.
Harold Robbins.
Unipart Calendars.
Kerb crawling.
Hanging.
Flagellation.
Personal videos.
Nudie neckties.
Exchange & Mart attire/advertisements.
Waterbeds.
Poppers.

BODY LANGUAGE

Cool people always sleep angelically on their fronts exposing just a hint of naked shoulder. Cool people always exude health and vitality in bath robes. Cool people always look stunning on the tennis court. Cool people always have cute little appendix scars. Cool people always win at arm (and leg) wrestling.

Body language is the one the Cools are all into. The body, the face, the arms, the legs. All the practised but natural looking movements. Here they all conspire to produce the knockout punch.

Body language is one of the best kept secrets of cool. Using what you've got, playing down what you haven't, making it all work for you.

How do the Cools do it?

First they take a part of the body
It could be a Jack Nicholson/Brooke Shields eyebrow.
A Bruce Weber/Victoria Principal chest.
A Brando forearm.
A Veronica Lake haircut.
A Paul Newman pair of eyes.
A Sandie Shaw foot.
A Sigourney Weaver nose.
A Debby Harry upper lip.
A Rachel Ward/Sean Connery voice.
Claire's knee.
Luke's cool hand.
Some of Chopin's fingers.
Anyone's ears, apart from Clark Gable's.

Then they use it

They raise an eyebrow in innocence, or they use it to look angry, or manic. They use their eyes to undress. Their hands to help. Their noses crinkle for attention. Their hair begs to be touched (she ran her fingers through his hair. Was it Brylcreem or hadn't it been washed for six weeks? By now she was too carried away to care).

They use their tongues to moisten upper lips in a kind of sexual expectation. Either that, or to seek out some non-existent crumb in the corner of their mouths to register absolute boredom.

The Cools are practised in the use of the deep sigh and the exhaled breath. The former implying need, the latter satisfaction.

The fingers are used to rub a temple, to remove a strand of hair, stroke a moustache or beard, or touch a G spot.

Their mouths. Grimly closed for the guitar solo or the chaste kiss. Wide open for the hard passionate tonsil-hoovering-kind-of-kiss or to give an unstifled yawn on being informed they've won the Booker Prize.

The knee that's desperate to be caressed. That doesn't react when it's hit hard with a surgical hammer to test reaction.

The foot that walks across burning coals or a rocky beach without registering a flicker of pain. The foot that's gainfully employed to karate kick a crumbling Tower Hamlets mansion block. The foot that wanders a little too far, but doesn't get sent back.

Then they add to it

It could be perfume. It could be an aftershave. A soupçon of motorway grime. A gallon of clean sweat (so clean you could drink it). A subtle emission of pheromones. Perhaps it's just a dash of eye makeup. Or plenty of exceptionally raunchy underwear under a totally demure exterior. Whatever it is they add, the Cools are always careful about how much they add and what brand it is. That brings us to the question of fashion accessories. But first, the customary hit list.

UNCOOL BODY LANGUAGE

- Farting – like Royalty, the Cools don't.
- Spitting – unlike the corporate French the Cools don't.
- Greasy hair – better a Yul or a Telly than this.
- Ear partings.
- Blackheads and whiteheads.
- Picking toenails and discarding the remains.
- Picking toenails and consuming the remains.
- Trying to pull your brain through your nose with right forefinger, ie picking your nose.
- Rubbing your crutch. (Men and women.)
- Trying surreptitiously to extract your underwear from your bum as you stroll casually down the high street.
- Wearing jeans that expose half your bum as you engage in manual labour.
- Mooning.
- Pulling large chunks of dead skin out of the unkempt brush that is your hair, examining them in a slightly perplexed manner and dropping them casually on someone else's persian rug.
- Removing wax from your inner ear with a paper clip during board meetings.
- Smiling with smoker's teeth.
- Throwing-up between courses in a nouvelle cuisine restaurant.
- Exhaling the remains of last night's chicken vindaloo when greeting Royals after the Command Performance.
- Biting your fingernails down to your knuckles.
- Hawking a trail along the high street the morning after you quit smoking.

THE PACKAGING. The icing on the cake. Important but not vital. The practitioner of cool doesn't need any help. With fashion the less said, the better. Go with the understatement.

Naturally, there aren't any rules. Anything goes as long as it's got the look. Street fashion is dead. Body consciousness means zilch. Clones are clowns.

There's day wear, night wear, summer wear, winter wear and underwear. There's the dark side and the light.

If you want something no expense should be spared.

Miz Cool likes her fashion but she ain't no Paloma Picasso.

Mr. Cool can live with it or without it. He's equally laid back in Levis as he is terrific in Tricot.

Many a cool image has been blown by the wrong threads. At the mere mention of the word 'tanktop' does a wry smile gather at the corners of your mouth? Well does it punk? . . .

MR. COOL'S WARDROBE

He has many personalities and they all like to dress up once in a while.

He can do a Brando *Streetcar Named Desire* no problem. All jeans, ripped T Shirts and bottled beer. Or a Jimmy Dean – all Harringtons, neatly pressed colour T-shirts, 501s, weejuns and metal combs.

He likes Anthony Price, Georgio Armani, and J.P. Gaultier when he's feeling Ferry and flash. And he slips effortlessly into Miami-vice-is-nice-but-Versace-is-better if the occasion requires it.

He knows all about silk and linen outfits courtesy of Nino Cerruti and Verri Uomo. He knows his Calvin Klein underwear and his Piatelli socks. After all he was wearing all that stuff long before Don Johnson and Phil Thomas came along. And yet when it comes down to it he isn't really all that bothered. A clean sweep of his wardrobe reveals that there are only a few real essentials he'd rather not live without.

THE ESSENTIAL TOGS

Levi 501s
Shrink to fit. Button flies. Red label. Red stitching on inside leg.

Popularised by the working men of the California gold rush as well as the mods of the mid-sixties. These jeans have been around since 1850 and continue to travel the 66 routes of every popular western culture.

If you can't find a pair of these in the wardrobe forget everything. Essentially there should be at least three pairs. One pair blue-newish. One pair faded to a nice three year tan. And one pair hanging by a thread (three to ten years).

Pity they've started advertising again since every dodo will soon be wanting a pair – 'Oh look, Lorraine, it's those funny old jeans you used to have to shrink in the bath. I thought they went out years ago. I suppose I better get a pair in case I miss out'.

Nevertheless 501s are up there with the gods, with little likelihood of ever losing their appeal.

Their pre-shrunken orange labelled half-brothers are frequently misconceived as being cut of the same cool cloth. They aren't and never will be.

Panama hat
A superb example of vernacular design, this one is attractive, durable and entirely practical. It can be rolled up to fit in the pocket and unrolled without problem. A word of caution however – beware of looking like a Botham clone.

A pair of chuck taylor converse sneakers
Tough as old boots these last. Throw them in the laundry and they come bouncing out, good as new.

A striped Henley blazer
Worn with jeans, a collarless white cotton shirt, and a couple of days stubble. Dressed like this, people will suspect you're a front man of a first division recording group (ie a rockstar).

A cricket jumper
For the Dairy Box/Weekend look – ie where they use starburst filters to make the river sparkle. Plenty of white clothing, sunsilk hair and smiling summer faces. Cricket jumpers are usually hung around the neck or waist but rarely worn. The short sleeved variety is becoming more preferred among the cool cricketing fraternity.

Church's brogues (two pairs)
One black. One brown. Most models except the totally grandad and the military look. This stylish footwear is built to last and can be worn both with fatigues and finery.

Argyle socks
Various colours. Various permutations. Every time you buy a pair, chuck an old nylon pair out. Don't ask why. Just do it.

Boxer shorts
For the movie star military look. These are good for giving a little paunch covering, an area where Eminence always falls down.

Endless supply of T shirts
Black and white – 100% cotton. The thin crisp American type – not the English nylony cotton type.

Dunlop green flash pumps
In good condition these can go with virtually anything. In bad condition they're ideal for creating that authentic Ramones look. All cheap, ripped and nasty.

A canvas ski-jacket
Very warm. Plenty of hidden pockets to hide your Zippos, Lucky Strikes, vitamin E tablets, Deutschmarks, chewing gum, Opinel pocket knives, Geiger counters and any miniature gadgets 'Q' might have asked you to test whilst on holiday.

Paul Smith

13-41 Floral Street, Covent Garden, London, WC2E 9DJ, England, Tel: 01-379-7133
23 Avery Row, London, W1X 9HD, England, Tel: 01-493-1287
10 Byard Lane, Nottingham NG1 2GJ, England, Tel: (0602) 506712
Warehouse, Stanford House, 6 Stanford Street, Nottingham, NG1 7BQ, England.
Tel: (0602) 505523, Telex 377258 Smith G.

A suggestion of Paul Smith

A name to splash out on. Reflecting a trend back to englishness. Suits, shirts, jackets, trousers, ties, cuff links, etc.

Climbing socks

Worn around the home hanging off the feet without shoes. They go with that 'I've-just-got-out-of-bed-after-a-three-day-party' look.

Two black leather jackets

One biker (Lewis). One soft, fashionable and expensive.

Cowboy shirt

Worn with tuxedos rather than wrangler jackets.

I'D RATHER BE DEAD THAN SEEN IN THAT

Playboy designer image wear

The ones with the funny logos all over the place, or the ones that say FU, or the ones with that sweet snappy little crocodile.

Message T shirts

'Bruce Wembley '85', 'Motorhead I.Q.42', 'Dylan Isle of Wight', or 'My parents went to Katmandu but all I got was this lousy T shirt' – anything in fact with a message on it. Worse still *Film 82, 83, 84, 85, 86* shirts, since it's uncool to respond to quizzes.

The odd exceptions are film production company T-shirts.

Grey shoes

Grey shoes don't make it with anything even if they're made of the most expensive leather. Oxfam might just take them off your hands if they're desperate.

Gucci

Gucci goes the same way as Sushi and Fiorucci, ie in the bin.

Anoraks (especially ones with Duckhams and other motoring logos on them)

'I'm only a gas station attendant but everyone thinks I work for the Emerson Fittipaldi racing team.' Dream on sucker.

£600 suits

Up to £599.99 O.K., but that's as far as it goes.

Pens in top pocket

Computer programmer. Civil Servant. Swotty student. Director of a mental institute.

'The shirt hanging out' look

If you must look like a twat wear flairs and platforms.

Shirt tucked into underpants

You get lucky with a girl. You go to the doctor for a check-up. You get run over by a milk float. Sooner or later someone's gonna find out.

Roll neck sweaters with buttons at the side

Yes there are still! one or two out there that Schwarzenegger hasn't yet terminated. Whatever happened to Simon Dee incidentally?

White Y-fronts

Especially the ones two sizes too big with plenty of natural ventilation.

String vests

Very Torremolinos. The perfect complement to knotted hanky sunguards, rolled-up strides, fish and chip suppers and Brut aftershave.

Cheesecloth shirts

See the buttons stretch. See the paunch strain.

Wearing a suit with sneakers

Print reps. Block makers. Failed civil servants. Mass murderers.

Male jewellery

None should be worn except perhaps a watch, a signet or a wedding ring. Avoid at all costs huge hoops, brass bangles and bravura brooches. Mummy's boys all.

Tattoos

L.o.v.e./H.a.t.e. written on alternate hands. A sorry looking dragon on the bum. 'I luv Mavis' on the neck. And worst of all – 'Made In England' stamped on the forehead.

The best tattoos are ex-ones since they leave such amazing scars.

Spotted ties worn with check shirts

ie Americans.

MIZ COOL'S WARDROBE

Miz Cool dresses for herself, not her man.

Miz Cool likes her clothes, but she's anything but a fashion victim. What's a fashion victim? Anyone who buys labels without any understanding. Anyone who would rather have a dress than pay the gas bill. Anyone who is obsessed by fashion but doesn't enjoy it.

Miz Cool has no time for fashion victims. *Dynasty*, The Emmanuels, Royal weddings are all an irrelevance. Joan, Britt, Liz, Nancy, Di and Krystle – if it wasn't

for the Heathrow photographer they wouldn't bother. But they do. And how.

Miz Cool is more at home with the Mrs Furillo look (one of the Captain's collarless shirts is good enough for her to wear around the home), or the casual cuts of Charlotte Rampling, Kathleen Turner, Sophia Loren and Meryl Streep. Like Miz Cool these don't have to try at all. They all know they could wear an old moth-eaten potato sack – minus the potatoes natch – and still look stunning.

When the occasion demands it, Miz Cool can don the elegant cool allure of a Grace Kelly (tailored clothes, Hermés scarves and real diamonds) or the catwalk cruise of a New York model at the Paris fashions.

Like Mr., Miz is comfortable in many guises.

Not so long ago she tended towards a war-like physique with a strongly defined narrow silhouette with aggressive shoulders. However, big and baggy once out now seems to be returning. The trend also seems to be swinging back to English conservative values, which means the elegant and traditional above all else. But Miz Cool is only too aware that like everything else in fashion, it's only a temporary phase.

At the moment she's into fetishist frills and her hair worn slick and sleek. Tomorrow, who knows? She might just stay in bed all day.

CURRENT OPTIONS

Colour black

Blackmail. Black Magic. Black sheep. 'Black is Black'. 'Paint it Black'.

Black is the camouflage of the Eighties. Many Miz Cools are reverting back to minimalism after being spoiled for choice for so long. Black is ideally suited. Black conjures up night, mystery, the outcast soul.

Buy a dress, a calculator, a radio or a penknife and you'll find that someone has issued a universal edict: any colour so long as it's black. Miz Cool actually doesn't give a flying fuck at the moon about all this, it just so happens she likes black. She likes colours too. Blue, red, green, yellow, pink, brown, orange.

Colour white

The understated angelic power of cool white linens, creamy white cardigans, slacks and cricket sweaters. Looks that go so well with summer, Gatsby lawns, and polo people. White is making its comeback, ever optimistic of the English summer.

Country Jap

Issey Miyake. Yohji Yamamoto. Kenzo.

Miyake is known as 'the architect of fashion'. Not only does he clothe 50,000 Sony workers in his jackets which at the touch of a zip are turned into waistcoats, he can take a worn linen rag which at the tug of a waistcord can be transformed into an infinitely flattering and expensive dress. Miz Cool likes Miyake because she believes that good design should look like no design. Clothes should express the body inside not cover it up.

The Beat route

Coffee-culture centres. The Beats are currently in favour. All polonecks, roll-necks, hoop earrings and midriff tied shirts. Rifat Ozbeck is the name to get your tongue around. A click of the finger. A burst of the sax, and go man, go.

Why should the fetishists have all the fun?

Black leather we know about. Rubber is daring, de Sadian and distinctly devo. It is essentially worn at parties, fashionable nightclubs or when casting a Helmut Newton fantasy. Miz Cool knows that with rubber plenty of talc should be used, and she is kind enough to tell less fortunate sisters that a spare tyre underneath won't help.

PVC

Last seen in the Sixties, PVC is now easier to wear especially when cuf-

COOL

Mr Cool: Jack Nicholson.

COOL

Miz Cool: Kathleen Turner.

fed, frilled and worked with lace and organza. The PVC look reflects the baby doll night-life sophistication of an early Catherine Deneuve. Throw in a couple of pairs of black high heels for good measure.

Forces' favourite
Original uniforms, particularly summer ones, with plenty of white linen. Miz Cool likes their quality and durability. The finish is first class, the seams don't split and the buttons stay on.

Madonna-ish
Virgin on the questionable cool. This one shouldn't be taken too seriously and certainly not beyond the age of twenty-two. Show plenty of underwear, lace and heavy chunky jewellery. If you can get away with it, without embarrassment, you have what it takes.

Azzedine Alia
Siren sculpted, sensual, accentuating the female form. Worn with demure elegance or outrageous sexuality.

Scott Crolla
Brocade and imperial finery. A Sixties flavour imbued with offbeat traditionalism.

Calvin Klein
Pure, understated. Luxury fabrics turn ultra-casual clothes, based on traditional sportswear separates,

into something very special. Once again, the accent is on countryside Englishness.

Jasper Conran
For his excellent design and mature look.

Chanel
For cashmere and Karl Lagerfeld.

John Rocha
For his cool assurance and a cool cut.

John Richmond/Maria Cornegio
For their exciting new breed of street fashion.

Jean Paul Gaultier
For his pinstripes and suits.

And well considered arrangements of Georgio Armani, Ralph Lauren and Katherine Hamnett.

MORE SHRIEK THAN CHIC
(BET LYNCH ON A
BERNI INN DATE)

- Black bra/white shirt.
- Bra straps on view.
- Tall person/flat shoes.
- Yellow stockings.
- Fringe boots.
- VPL (visible pantie line).
- Halter-neck dresses.

- Pop socks especially worn with dresses and skirts.
- Rings on every finger.
- Gold name chains.
- Studs through the nose (especially if you're prone to heavy mucoid colds).
- See-through dresses where the underskirt doesn't reach the hem.
- False eyelashes.

- Skinny-anorexia (everything falls off).
- Black lipstick.
- White shoes/black stockings.
- Long straight hair.
- Long false fingernails (overtones of Bela Lugosi in *Nosferatu*).
- Hair pieces.
- Hair spray (one match and 'woof').
- Hot-pants.
- Mink and rabbit jogging suits courtesy of Hermès.
- Stressed clothing – 'rip-off' rips .
- Gloria Vanderbilt designer wear.
- The Skinhead Look (combat jacket, black boots and braces on the trousers).
- The Greenham Common Look (combat jacket, green boots and braces on the teeth).

COOL Accessories After the Fact

ADJUNCTS. Additional things to the individual state. The true practitioner of purist cool doesn't really need any artefacts, but occasionally a few things borrowed are acceptable especially if they help to accentuate the refrigerated state.

Once again, let us take the example the slob-hero in *Diva*. Immeasurably cool because he lives such an uncluttered existence. He takes long leisurely baths in the centre of a large open, sparsely furnished room, and cooks with a chef's relish in a cubby-hole kitchen. Yet his oceanic jigsaw puzzle when he's a brooding Hamlet, and his matching twin pair of white Citroën Light 15s when he springs into action, are the powerful symbols that raise his slob-cool performance above Tom Waitsian levels.

Accessories can help both Mr. and Miz Cool in many ways. Sometimes a carefully chosen object will not only enhance their persona it will actually make it.

Where would the frisbee thrower be without his frisbee? Bogart without his Lucky Strikes? Clint without his Colts?

Where indeed?

Cool accessories have an appeal that sets them, like their owners, apart. Mass-produced but distinguishable from the mass. Expensive perhaps. Rare even. But either way, a powerful enough claim for their owners to be separate, sophisticated and cool.

The cigarette

This Freudian artefact practically deserves a chapter of its own. To many smoking is questionable cool. Certainly it should be given up by the age of forty.

In the meantime stick with the French, Gitanes and Gauloises, or obscure foreign brands – Russian, Turkish. Camels untipped are OK, since the packs are as important as the smoke. Plus they give your voice that extra 'throaty' appeal. Generally soft packs are in, hard are out.

OTHER COOL BRANDS Marlboro Lites, St Moritz, Chesterfield, Players untipped, Kent. Fribourg and Treyer. Davidoffs. Pall Mall.
UNCOOL BRANDS Rothmans, B&H, Piccadilly, Dunhill, Silk Cut blues and reds, Embassy blues and reds. Woodbines. Lambert and Butler. John Player Special. Capstan Full Strength. No. 6. (Number anything.) Sobranie Cocktail. Park Drive. More. Roll your own.

Famous smokers are legendary –

Bogart. Bacall. Bowie. The collective French cinema who utilize their lower lips to talk and smoke at the same time. There's Dietrich and Dylan. Private eyes. Guitar players of the 'Clapton/Richard/Ron Wood' school who use their fret-boards as holders. The mean cattle-coated cheroot smok-

ers of the Clint creche. The elegant society models of the Twenties, who did it the Vogue way with cigarette holders. Paul Henreid and Bette Davis did it à-deux when they had the stars but lacked the moon.

Non-smokers James Cagney, Spencer Tracy, Warren Beatty all had to draw on alternative material to strengthen their characters.

Ashtrays are cool, especially if French. The blue and yellow Ricard, preferably an original. And basically anything nicked from Parisian restaurants, or which carry original advertising messages on them.

Matches are Swan Vestas or the 'book' variety from American hotels and cocktail bars in the Los Angeles and New York areas.

Zippo lighter

Designed by George Blaisdell in 1932 this chunky lighter has a hinged top, and a wick surrounded by a windhood so you don't blow it when lighting a cigarette. A standard issue amongst U.S. GIs in WW2 it's still highly classy today. It has a nostalgic rugged charm that affords its owner a leisured, eyecatching Chandleresque appeal when lighting up.

Rayban Wayfarers

With a black pair of these anyone can look like Jack Nicholson or Christie Brinkley.

Rayban Aviator shades

The romance of the aviators is renewed as they emerge from their English countryside aerodromes once again. Popularized by the fur-jacketed U.S. fly boys of WW2, their teardrop shape was determined by functional principles to correspond exactly to the eye's field of vision (ie to fit). The quality of the Bausch and Lomb lenses are designed to protect the eye, making the wearer 'look good' as well as 'see good'. American cops, sportsmen and political assassins are particularly partial to these shades.

Cutler and Gröss glasses

A slightly reflective plastic type of shade (NB ski and other reflective glasses being passé as fashion accessories). High-tech circles, rivets and oil slick lenses. Art directors, designers and Sunday Times colour-supp readers are partial to these.

Sony Walkman

Mozart in the privacy of your own head.

The finer musical principles of a Bolivian flute ensemble privately making your audience nauseous on a crowded tube train. An essential beach accoutrement. An item of modern jewellery.

Walkman users are elevated above the miserable, downtrodden throng. You see a mundane urban landscape and it suddenly takes on

the appearance of your directorial film debut – a social comment without words, just your carefully selected soundtrack. Warning: while enjoying a cerebral tune or two it's v.v. uncool to suddenly break into song or a Nils Lofgren routine.

Rolex Oyster Perpetual

Not possessing a watch is cool. But if you must have one make it an old one of these. Forget Cartier, screw Audemars-Piguet. This is the real McCoy.

Dating back as early as 1910 when anything other than a pocket-watch was considered faggy, the oyster is a classic that transcends fashion. Quality and function are more important than looks or technology. Ask any deep sea diver, astronaut or airman.

Pentax Spotmatic or ESII Camera

One manual, the other automatic exposure, these two basic models and their variations are minor classics of photographic art, and have yet to be exceeded in terms of looks and toughness. Popularized by the Bailey brigade of London fashion photographers of the Sixties they still give excellent results today and lend an air of professionalism to their owners. They coolly disdain the unnecessary technological advances that glut the amateur market of today. Like the early VW Beetles and Citroën 2CVs these go on and on and the cachet of owning one grows accordingly.

Polaroid SX70 Land camera

Polaroid culture is still cool despite the overkill afforded it by Hockney, Warhol and the ex-Japan lead singer David Sylvian. This is by far the best (now deleted) model. Auto focus. Superb quality of reproduction. It's good for recording visitors and celebrities to your home.

Any Leica camera whatsoever

Whether it's an old rangefinder or a modern SLR these are probably the most expensive, certainly the best lenses (Leitz) money can buy.

Mont Blanc pen

Although deliberately antiquarian in appearance, the exclusive Mont Blanc Meisterstuck fountain pen has become a huge international success as a prized cult object.

Fender Stratocaster

If you want to be Eric, Jimi (white left-handed), Rory, Nils, Mark, Hank, etc. – get one of these. Pre 1962 models are best (the company got taken over by CBS). Accept no Jap substitute, however superior.

Fender Telecaster

If you want to be Keith, Bruce, Francis, Chrissie, etc., these create a 'tinnier' sound than the above and are generally used by more 'desperate' rockers. Once again, pre-1962 models are best. Accept no substitute other than a Leo G.

Any Martin accoustic guitar

The earlier the better. Handmade American craftsmanship. Effing expensive. Either one of these or a round-backed Ovation.

Guinness mug

Want a pint of Guinness? Need a proper mug, John.

Luger Automatic

As used by Kraut officers in WW2 and in different versions before. These fine pistols look like the best in Bauhaus design even though the heavy magnums of today make them seem like peashooters by comparison.

Umbrella
For Gentleman Jim Cool, or for Slob Cool, umbrellas add that vital touch of class. Plus the fact that Cools with wet hair aren't so cool. (In London get them hand-made at Smiths in New Oxford Street.)

Victorinox Swiss army knife
The designer knife that does everything, from breaking into a Swiss bank vault to opening a tin of caviare.

Durabeam torch
Used with Duracel batteries. The flip-top works as a switch, but can also be used to direct the beam of light if the torch is used in a free standing position.

A word processor
You got a book to write? A screenplay? A quick venomous communication to your bank manager? A note for your milkman? Then forget buying a dishwasher, get one of these. It spells, it corrects, it lines up – it does everything apart from make tea, and the keyboard sounds just like you're hacking a bank fraud. What more could you ask for?

Oriental girl (or boy) friend
Mick, Keith, Woodsy, Rod and the odd Duran Duran may have American counterparts but with world focus shifting to Europe and the East orientals can make cool mates.

Cash
Wads. Bill folds. Rolls. Best used for bribes – the £20 note in the top pocket followed by a playful slap. Tips – Hey. Keep the change. Hey. Don't mention it. After all you earned it, so you've a right to see it go. Apparently the Americans don't use it anymore (apart from the odd $1 million ransoms carried in small attaché cases) which is a shame.

And, of course, the odd **Braün** artefact.

UNCOOL ACCESSORIES – THE ALBATROSS ROUND THE NECK SYNDROME

- Diamond in the tooth – worse still an emerald because everyone will think you've got a piece of spinach stuck to your tooth.
- Pen around neck – the holiday courier look.
- Belt key rings – so you've got more than one front door key, big deal.
- Sex aids – the Cools don't need them, especially those of the chemical variety.
- Filofax – I'm creative. I'm in films. I'm in an expensive restaurant.
- *Financial Times* – No comment.
- Beeping 'where are my bloody' keys.
- Beeping 'It's time I took my pill' watches. Especially *uncool* in crowded, silent theatres.
- Car alarms – especially on Datsuns no-one wants to steal in the first place.
- Credit cards – 'let's burn plastic. Yeah why not.' The worst offender is a Gold American Express card. So what if you can buy the crown jewels – you've still got to pay it back.
- Carrier bags.
- Badges.
- I.D. bracelets – 'My name's Dave. But in case I forget I got it written on me wrist.'
- Gold neck chains – 'My bird finks

I look like one of the Bee Gees.'
- S&M gear – by night a wild defiant immoral soul. By day an accountant.
- Crappy suitcases – there is nothing worse than a crappy suitcase. Check out Louis Vuitton for the best.
- Dunhill accessories.
- Anything with personal initials –

even your silk pyjamas.
- Reproduction Bauhaus building blocks.
- Kipper ties – their only redeeming feature is covering up major spillage, ie gravy and custard stains.
- Digital watches – 65p for twelve. OK 57p for the lot.
- Fag behind earhole – 'No I'm not working class, I'm actually trying to improve my pool playing look.'
- Pocket calculators – especially when brought out in restaurants to decide everyone's share of the bill.
- Brolly hats – £2.85 on Oxford Street. 'A real snip, and you don't have to carry a thing.' You may keep dry but that's no excuse for looking like an extra-testicle.
- Gold sovereign signet rings.
- Walking along the street with a cellular phone.
- Luncheon vouchers – especially paying a huge restaurant bill with four thousand of them and expecting change if it doesn't exactly match up.
- Silver brandy glass warmers.
- Steering wheel covers.
- Sunlamps.
- Tablets that give you a suntan.
- Swatch watches. Questionable cool since by 1989 two thirds of the Western hemisphere will own one.
- Mittens. Especially worn in hot weather.
- 'I love' stickers.

COOL

MOVIES

THE MORE you see, the better. The more you know, the better. Movies are where the Cools would ideally be. Movie buffs each and every one, they know all there is to know about directors, their films, plots, key dialogue, selected foreign oeuvres, Ealing comedies, early Altman, the best of Bunuel, the new Aussie flix. It pays to know who were the key-grips, best boys and gaffers in the more important pictures. Cools can reel off with consummate ease the exact moments when Hitchcock appears and The Lady Vanishes.

They know something of the lives of the stars. They amuse themselves with Anger's *Hollywood Babylon* and Goldman's *Adventures in the Screen Trade*. But essentially, it's the celluloid product that matters.

Their multiple video systems work slavishly day and night, recording films noirs of the Forties or keeping up to date with the current Eighties crop.

The Cools generally hate cinemas which is a bit of a problem since that is generally where films are shown. Poor sound quality, out-of-focus picture, and faded prints are a constant source of irritation. As are chatty couples, popcorn addicts and cheering prats who think that the movie is actually real life. Complaints to managers

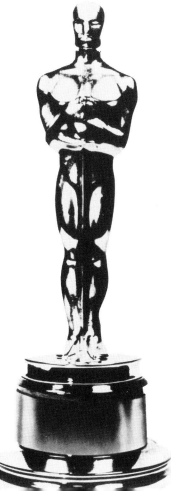

simply result in offers of cut price tickets for *Death Wish 4* as compensation. Next year's cheque for the NFT membership is therefore already in the post. On leaving a cinema the Cools never discuss the film until they're far away from the crowd. It's very uncool to express cinematic comments for no other reason than to try and impress other cinema goers. 'It was OK but I found it very derivative of Bergman's early work, without any of the wit. His last film, on the other hand. . .'

The Cools have their special favourites which they've seen several times over. They've got whole movies complete with dialogue on constant screening in their head, and on occasion will blend normal day to day speak with some favourite lines. Eg *'Go ahead. Make my day'; 'Take the chicken and hold it between your knees'; 'I've been killing spiders since I was thirty. OK'; 'Here's looking at you, kid'; 'I'm asking you to marry me, you little fool'*, etc.

Movies, no matter how old are a great source of cool ideas and adopted personas. How to drink. How to smoke. How to cut to the quick. How to treat members of the opposite sex. How to deal with low-life. How to play three-card brag. How to mix a cocktail shaken not stirred. Even how to converse with a bank robber after foiling his robbery: *'I know what you're think-*

COOL

ing. Did he fire six shots or only five? Well, to tell you the truth. in all this excitement I've kinda lost track myself. But being that this is a .44 magnum, the most powerful hand-gun in the world, and would blow your head clean off – you've got to ask yourself one question: do I feel lucky? Well do ya, punk?'

Sooner or later, somewhere, somehow the Cools will bring a little movie dialogue into their con-versation. The trick is to know it and to spot it.

As a rule, the Cools love everything there is to love about movies. There is only one excep-tion, apart from bad movies, and that is when movie people make assholes of themselves in public.

ACADEMY AWARD UNCOOL

Since there's no business like show business, some film people let the occasion go completely to their heads and go totally overboard on sentimental assholery when they win an Oscar.

It's hard to choose between Colin Welland's tough northern grit-ty *'The British are coming'* and Sally Field's shrieky, squawky *'You really like me!'* for total embarrassment. Since everyone knows that only films with unpronounceable (ie at least to the Americans) names like *Amadeus* and *Ghandi* directed by equally unpronounceable names like *Sir Richard Atten-burrow* and *My-Loss-Four-Man* win Oscars

you'd think they'd be forever trying to film the life story of the *Dalai Lama* or *Leo-Nard Nimoy.*

ACADEMY AWARD COOL

'What do I want with another doorstop?'
(ALFRED HITCHCOCK)

Not winning is cool. Spielberg, Hitchock, Paul Newman, Edward G. Robinson, have never won one. (Newman and Hitchcock only got one for services to the industry.)

Rejecting them is cool too. Brando sent Shasheen Little-feather to reject his 1971 Oscar for *The Godfather* on his behalf while he campaigned for the Sioux at Wounded Knee. No more Oscars for him until the movies quit casting Red Indians as the villains. George C. Scott followed his exam-ple. Woody Allen who won 3 Oscars for *Annie Hall*, didn't turn up for the ceremony because it clashed with his Dixieland night at Michael's Pub in New York.

THE FIRST
ONE-HUNDRED

■ **Casablanca (1942 Director Michael Curtiz)** Bogart and Berg-man at their best. Rick's Café. Rick's chick. WW2. Master cast. Master technicians. This one just

fell together perfectly, although at the time, no one, not even the director, knew how it would end.

■ **The Big Sleep (1946 Director Howard Hughes)** Complicated, moody thriller whose author (Chandler) admitted that even he couldn't say 'who done it'. Great script. Great performance. Great fun.

■ **The Maltese Falcon (1941 Director John Huston)** A group of assorted characters hunt the Mal-tese Falcon. Greenstreet, Lorre, et al. Bogart demonstrates how to treat a lady (Mary Astor) when she doesn't play square with him. She has to take a fall because he won't play the sap for her.

■ **The Godfather (1971 Director Francis Ford Coppola)** The wed-ding. The 'I made him an offer he couldn't refuse'. The Horse's head. The betrayals and counter be-trayals. Grand scale Mafia movie that demonstrates the important of family loyalty. Cappice.

■ **Godfather 2 (1974 Director Francis Ford Coppola)** The bril-liant sequel. The bits before. The bits after. Pacino's best perform-ance. 'You're my brother Fredo and I love you but don't ever take sides against the family or I'll blow your brains out.'

■ **Blade Runner (1982 Director Ridley Scott)** From the novel *Do Androids Dream of Electric Sheep* by Philip K. Dick. A futuristic private eye thriller with Harrison Ford as Marlowe. Full of moody atmosphere and beautiful co-stars. Sean Young as the love interest, Rutger Hauer as the baddie android with some of the best delivered lines in the cinema and Daryl Hannah as his mannequin girlfriend.

■ **Alien (1979 Director Ridley Scott)** The eerie opening titles. This one puts the frighteners on from the word go. A much misunderstood movie. Like most of Scott's work, it should be seen more than once to gain full effect. One of the most erotic scenes in the cinema occurs when Sigourney changes out of and straight back into her space suit for her final confrontation with the creature. ☞

■ **The Duellists (1977 Director Ridley Scott)** Keith Carradine/ Harvey Keitel conduct a series of duels over 16 years in the early 1800s. Stunning period piece that makes excellent use of a thin plot, despite looking like a TV commercial.

■ **Bonnie & Clyde (1967 Director Arthur Penn)** Sleepy mid America at the time of America's most feared bank robbers. Cool couple Beatty and Dunaway start a trend in fashionable violence.

■ **Angel (1982 Director Neil Jordan)** Stephen Rea in metaphysical IRA thriller. His saxophonist is drawn into a maze of violence when he avenges the murder of mute female fan.

■ **Angels with Dirty Faces (1938 Director Michael Curtiz)** Low budget. Fast talking gangster movie with Cagney as hero to juvenile

street gang. Great ending. (See *Dying to be cool*.)

■ **Blow-Up (1966 Director Michelangelo Antonioni)** Brash Swinging Sixties photographer David Hemmings doing a David Bailey discovers everything is not what it seems. This one perfectly captures the best black and white Pentax creative mood of the period.

■ **Assault on Precinct 13 (1976 Director John Carpenter)** Electric electronic exploitation movie. Tension built up beautifully as police station comes under siege. Cool couple 'lifer' and girl intermittently lighting each other cigarettes as they waste legions of crazed Kamikaze gang members.

■ **Philadelphia Story (1950 Director George Cukor)** Cary Grant, Katharine Hepburn, James Stewart in fast-paced, fast-talking upper class weekend wedding of the rich but not so stupid. Later remade as *High Society*.

■ **His Girl Friday (1940 Director Howard Hawks)** No time to draw breath in this one. One of the best comedies ever. A remake of *The Front Page*. A gag every other second. Cary Grant, Rosalind Russell at their acid best.

■ **Performance (1970 Director Nicholas Roeg)** Fine performance from James Fox as sexually ambivalent East End thug who suffers an I.D. crisis after meeting up with Mick and Anita. Well who wouldn't?

■ **Don't Look Now (1973 Director Nicholas Roeg)** Donald Sutherland and Julie Christie in supernatural ESP thriller in Venice. Look out for the figure in the red coat.

■ **Solaris (1972 Director Andrei Tarkovsky)** SF ghost story as a phycologist is sent to investigate deaths at a space station.

■ **2001 A Space Odyssey (1968 Director Stanley Kubrick)** Unbeatable SF enigma. Lucy in the Sky with Diamonds? The sequel 2010 was quite passable but wasn't necessary.

■ **Dr. Strangelove (1963 Director Stanley Kubrick)** Peter Sellers plays three characters in this black cold war comedy. A mad USAF general launches a nuclear attack on Russia and then changes his mind.

■ **Chinatown (1974 Director Roman Polanski)** Like Hitchcock, Polanski appears briefly as a nose cutter. Jack Nicholson's private eye uncovers a very complicated conservationist mystery on the lines of *The Big Sleep*. John Huston in excellent form as grizzled old power monger.

■ **Point Blank (1967 Director John Boorman)** Violent modernist gangster movie. An elegy for old style hoodlum methods, as Lee Marvin, betrayed by partner and wife, takes revenge on the syndicate (all suited businessmen and luxury penthouses). Best scene — when his wife beats him up while he remains totally immovable.

■ **Ai No Corrida (1976 Director Nagisha Oshima)** An earlier one from Mr Merry Xmas Mr Lawrence. Erotic obsessions. Lovers go all the way literally. A sort of Japanese *Last Tango in Paris*.

■ **Winter Kills (1979 Director Richard Condon)** Intrigue, paranoia and political assassination of the JFK genre (see also Alan J. Pakula's *The Parallax View* and David Miller's *Executive Action*) with touches of black humour thrown in for good measure.

■ **Liquid Sky (1984 Director Slava Tsukerman)** A new wave model gets visited by an alien from outer space. The result? Anyone trying it on with her spells instant oblivion. Funny, perverse, erotic, intriguing.

■ **Five Easy Pieces (1970 Director Bob Rafelson)** A younger Jack Nicholson as a talented dropout who revisits the family homestead. Includes the immortal chicken salad sandwich lines.

■ **One Flew Over the Cuckoo's Nest (1975 Director Milos Foreman)** Based on a Ken Kesey book written some fourteen years earlier, it is both funny and horrifying. Set in a mental hospital, Jack Nicholson wins a highly-deserved Oscar for best manic stare. Great scenes: football on blank TV screen. The raise-your-hand scene. The big Indian. The denoument.

■ **Southern Comfort (1981 Director Walter Hill)** Eerie Ry Cooder slide-guitar music. Louisiana Indians battle it out with national guardsmen in swampland. Catch Powers Booth's amazing Zippo cigarette lighting technique.

■ **Body Heat (1981 Director Lawrence Kasdan)** Long hot sultry summer drags by as cool couple Kathleen Turner and William Hurt indulge in all manner of lust while plotting murder.

■ **All About Eve (1950 Director Joseph L. Mankiewicz)** Bette Davis, Anne Baxter in savage witty drama. Brilliant performances as an ageing Broadway star defends herself against up and coming ambitious young actress.

■ **Altered States (1980 Director Ken Russell)** William Hurt. A psychologist uses a sensory deprivation tank to hallucinate himself back into primitive states of human evolution, in which guise he emerges to kill. Heaveee.

■ **Mad Max 2 (The Road Warrior – US Title) (1981 Director George Miller)** Handsome Mel Gibson in much improved (over *Mad Max 1*) futuristic wasteland thriller. Spectacular and violent.

■ **A Matter of Life and Death (1946 Directors Michael Powell & Emeric Pressburger)** Very David Niven. Very British. Very stiff upper lip. Excellent story of 'dead' airman who goes to heaven only to plead for a return to earth and the woman he loves. A haunting piano scale score.

■ **Jeremiah Johnston (1972 Director Sydney Pollack)** Robert Redford as ice-cool trapper fighting and gaining respect of ice-cool injuns. Huntin' fishin' squawin', etc.

■ **Duel in the Sun (1946 Director King Vidor)** A half-breed girl causes trouble between two brothers – Gregory Peck and Joseph Cotten. The end scene when baddie lovers Peck and Jennifer Jones kill each other out of love is both cool and moving.

■ **Metropolis (1926 Director Fritz Lang)** Silent futuristic drama the style of which was borrowed by a recent Kelly Girl commercial. Workers in a modernistic state are

kept underground while unrest is quelled by a saintly girl, Maria. Mad inventor creates an evil 'Maria' android to incite revolt.

■ **Now Voyager (1942 Director Irving Rapper)** Bette Davis as frustrated spinster takes psychiatric cure and embarks on doomed love affair. The one with the great cigarette scene with the 'who needs the moon when we've got the stars' line.

■ **Bad Day at Black Rock (1954 Director John Sturges)** Seminal suspense thriller. A one-armed stranger, Spencer Tracy, gets off a train at a sleepy town and is greeted by hostility. The moments of violence, long awaited, are electrifying.

■ **Badlands (1973 Director Terence Malik)** A latterday Bonnie and Clyde with Martin Sheen and Sissy Spacek as dim witted juveniles on the run. Excellent music and directorial debut.

■ **Apocalypse Now (1979 Director Francis Ford Coppola)** Based on Conrad's *Heart of Darkness*. This one created the chaos and lunacy of Vietnam in the privacy of your local Odeon. ☛

■ **The Wild One (1954 Director Laslo Benedek)** Motorcycle gang terrorise a small town.

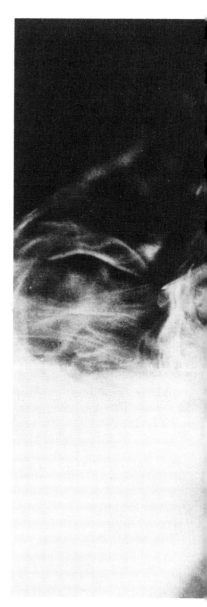

Fine nihilistic performance from Brando.

■ **The Private Life of Sherlock Holmes (1970 Director Billy Wilder)** The best of all the Sherlock Holmes films. Intriguing tripartite plot. And there's even a suggestion of women in it. Watson!

■ **Cool Hand Luke (1967 Director Stuart Rosenberg)** Sentenced to two years hard labour, a convict (Paul Newman) becomes a legend of invulnerability and a Christ figure to his chain gang mates.

■ **The Graduate (1967 Director Mike Nichols)** Highly amusing Californian pastiche of middle class life, where Hoffman as student falls for the daughter after an affair with the mother. Despite the era, it has hardly dated.

■ **The Outlaw Josey Wales (1976 Director Clint Eastwood)** Without a doubt Clint's best western. Avenging farmer takes a band of misfits through violent encounters into the promised land. Great supporting performance by Chief Dan George.

■ **Once Upon a Time in the West (1969 Director Serge Leone)** Notice the water images. Notice the cattle coats. Notice the sequence where mean Jack Elam traps a fly in his gun barrel. A western with a meaning.

■ **The Good, The Bad and The Ugly (1966 Director Serge Leone)** The way we dream all westerns should be. Evil grins. White teeth. Perfect beards. Sacks of coins. The fastest draws. And a civil war thrown in for good measure. Epic in all proportions.

■ **Once Upon a Time in America (1985 Director Serge Leone)** Jewish gangster chronicles. When Leone takes on a project he gives it his all. De Niro's acts. ☞

■ **Heaven's Gate (1980 Director Michael Cimino)** The biggest flop of all time. Actually it's quite excellent.

■ **The Big Chill (1983 Director Lawrence Kasdan)** A bunch of ex-college graduates re-unite after a mutual friend's suicide. They spend the weekend together and discover the changes that have occured over the previous 10 or 15 years. The sort of story you wish you'd written. Excellent Sixties soundtrack.

■ **The Last Picture Show (1971 Director Peter Bogdanovich)** Nostalgic black and white feel. Teenage affairs in small Texas town in 1951. It ends with the hero heading for Korea and the closing down of the local cinema.

■ **Annie Hall (1977 Director**

Woody Allen) Semi autobiographical Woody Allen comedy. He meets flighty girl (Diane Keaton) and educates her in the ways of the world. Once done she takes off for fame on the phoney west coast. He remains the wiser on the east coast.

■ **The Prisoner of Zenda (1937 Director John Cromwell)** Previously filmed in 1913 and 1922 and later in 1952 and 1979 this is by far the best version. Ronald Coleman in exhilarating form as the swashbuckling traveller mistaken for Royalty.

■ **The Third Man (1949 Director Carol Reed)** Hauntingly memorable and irresistible stylish romantic thriller perfectly capturing post war Vienna. The most famous theme tune ever and the immortal cuckoo-clock lines. A successful translation of German expressionist style.

■ **Citizen Kane (1941 Director Orson Welles)** The rise and fall of a newspaper tycoon. Orson's first film and finest two hours.

■ **Top Hat (1935 Director Mark Sandwich)** Astair and Rogers. Mistaken ID. Cheek to cheek. A great musical memory.

■ **Butch Cassidy and The Sundance Kid (1969 Director George** Roy Hill) One of the great buddy-buddy movies. Maximum excitement from minimum set pieces. The opening card game. The knife fight. The cycle ride. The long chase. Irresistible.

■ **Diva (1981 Director J. J. Beineix)** Flashy surreal thriller with cool central character. Generally overrated, but fascinating imagery. Opera. Drug smuggling. Subway chases. Lighthouse retreat. Mammoth jigsaw puzzle.

■ **Celine and Julie Go Boating (1974 Director Jacques Rivette)** Two women change the outcome of a drama played daily in a haunted house. Odd, dreamy mood piece with overtones of *Alice in Wonderland.*

■ **Rear Window (1954 Director Alfred Hitchcock)** Cool Grace Kelly as James Stewart's lady-friend who's more interested in a bit of fun than a murderous situation taking place in the apartment opposite.

■ **In the Heat of the Night (1967 Director Norman Jewison)** Steiger and Poitier battle it out to see who's coolest in this tale of murder set against deep south bigotry (ie hatred of blacks, ie Poitier).

■ **Pinocchio (1940 Director Walt Disney)** More fantastic than Fantasia. Puppet has to prove himself before he can turn into a real boy.

■ **Build My Gallows High (Out of the Past — US title) (Director Jacques Tourneur)** Cool director (*Night of the Demon, Cat People*). Bob Mitchum as detective falling for homicidal girl Jane Greer with violent consequences.

■ **The Wild Bunch (1969 Director Sam Peckinpah)** The first time the 'blood-spurt' technique was used. Sam's best movie chronicles the fate of old cowboy bankrobbers caught up in changing times. Hang on to your seat for the last twenty minutes.

■ **The President's Analyst (1967 Director Theodore J. Flicker)** James Coburn in wild political satirical farce which finally unmasks as its chief villain the phone company.

■ **Dirty Harry (1971 Director Don Siegel)** Tough detective brings mad (and I mean mad) sniper to book. Much-copied cop movie, with three endings.

■ **The Seven Samurai (1954 Director Akira Kurosawa)** The original magnificent seven. Magnificent, like most of Kurosawa's cinematic explorations.

■ **The Long Good Friday (1980 Director John MacKenzie)** Brilliant East London gangster film with Bob Hoskins as leader in and out of control. Powerful, frightening and real despite a few Sweeney overtones.

■ **Goldfinger (1964 Director Guy Hamilton)** Probably the liveliest of the Bonds. *Dr. No*, and *From Russia with Love* are also landmarks. The Sean Connery/Bond movies represent a whole era of cool. Mr. 'Raised Eyebrows' Roger Moore could never match Connery's suave acting.

■ **Le Boucher (1969 Director Claude Chabrol)** Charming slice of French small town drama. A series of murders are traced to the inoffensive local butcher who is courting the local mistress.

■ **Blood Simple (1985 Joel and Ethan Cohen)** Deep in the heart of Texas murder most foul. Brilliant first film by two brothers. Full of slow dark disturbing images and excellent characterisation, especially M. Emmet Walsh as the gumshoe.

■ **The Year of Living Dangerously (1982 Director Peter Weir)** Excellent political parable set in Indonesia with Mel Gibson, and Sigourney Weaver as the love interest, and Linda Hunt as the 'boy' friend.

■ **La Grande Illusion (1937 Director Jean Renoir)** In WW1 three captured French pilots have an uneasy relationship with their German Commandant. The meaning of war, mankind and more.

■ **Carrie (1976 Director Brian de Palma)** Repressed teenager with remarkable powers fakes revenge on bullying class mates. Great last scene. Just when you thought it was time to get the takeaway. ☞

■ **The Blues Brothers (1980 Director John Landis)** Dan Ackroyd, John Belushi. Enormously expensive cult-movie. A wacky comedy about two white spivs obsessed with Fifties R&B resulting in an epic chase through contemporary America.

■ **Saturday Night and Sunday Morning (1960 Director Karel Reisz)** Working class melodrama with strong comedy sides sees hero Albert Finney rebel against convention only to return. British cinema at its zenith.

■ **The General (1926 Director Buster Keaton)** One of the funniest silent comedies ever with Buster Keaton.

■ **Local Hero (1983 Director Bill Forsyth)** Gentle meaning of life comedy centred around American property speculator who arrives at sleepy Scots fishing village only to

COOL

be entranced by its magic spell.

■ Dead Men Don't Wear Plaid (1982 Director Carl Reiner) Cool comic Steve Martin in very clever and funny collage of Forties film and Thirties sequences intercut with modern day ones. The idea was successfully 'borrowed' for the Holsten Pils TV campaign. ☞

■ Belle de Jour (1967 Director Louis Bunuel) Fact and fantasy as doctor's wife (Catherine Deneuve) finds afternoon work in a brothel. The sort of thing the French do so well.

■ Seven Days in May (1964 Director John Frankenheimer) An American General's aide discovers his boss wants to take over the country because he finds the President's fascism traitorous.

■ The Seventh Seal (1957 Director Ingmar Bergman) Death comes to a knight who challenges him to a chess game while he, unsuccessfully, tries to show Death the goodness in mankind.

■ Slaughterhouse 5 (1972 Director George Roy Hill) Based on a Kurt Vonnegut novel. A suburban optometrist has nightmare space/time fantasies involving Nazi POW camps and a strange futuristic planet.

■ Battleship Potemkin (1925 Director Sergei Eisenstein) An episode of the 1905 revolution in Russia. A masterpiece of creative editing – the famous Odessa steps massacre. Voted the best film ever by an international panel in 1948 and 1958.

■ The Thomas Crown Affair (1968 Director Norman Jewison) Classy bank caper thriller. Bored rich man (McQueen) masterminds two identical bank robberies as girlfriend insurance investigator tries to snare him.

■ Bullitt (1968 Director Peter Yates) Splendid cop movie. The San Francisco car chase. Cool as a breeze. A busy year for McQueen.

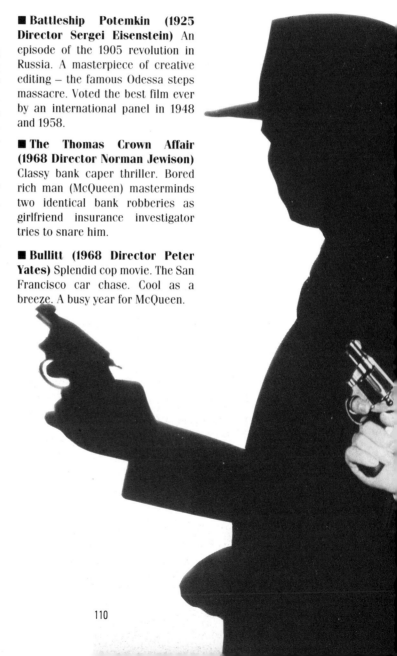

■ **Billy Liar (1963 Director John Schlesinger)** Brilliant urban Walter Mittyish comic fantasy set in Yorkshire. An undertakers clerk tries to escape his roots and almost succeeds.

■ **Midnight Cowboy (1969 Director John Schlesinger)** John Voight and Dustin Hoffman as down and out buddies eking out a precarious existence in the New York gutter.

■ **A Night at The Opera (1935 Director Sam Wood)** Marx Brothers wreck and then help an opera company. One of their best. Great musical interludes. See also *Duck Soup, Animal Crackers, A Day at the Races.*

■ **A Hard Day's Night (1964 Director Richard Lester)** A day in the life of The Beatles. Comic Sixties fantasia with music. The director tries every cinematic gag in the book. Successfully.

■ **Klute (1971 Director Alan J. Pakula)** Taut adult thriller with Jane Fonda and Donald Sutherland as beautifully cool couple. Him cop. She call girl.

■ **El Topo (1971 Director Alexandro Jodorowsky)** A gunfighter rides through the old west, has various encounters after which he sets himself on fire. The absurdity of life? Who knows?

favours of Janet Suzman.

■ **Lawrence of Arabia (1962 Director David Lean)** Beautiful spectacular epic with Peter O'Toole at his best as the mysterious historic figure. Amazing mirage-like first appearance of Omar Sharif.

■ **Great Expectations (1946 Director David Lean)** Superb rendering of popular Dickens novel.

■ **Singin' in The Rain (1952 Director Gene Kelly/Stanley Donen)** Weird, wonderful and wacky musical that's never been bettered.

■ **Brazil (1984 Director Terry Gilliam)** A clerk meets the girl of his dreams in a reality that seems like a dream. A highly original film from the director of the equally original *Time Bandits*.

■ **The French Connection 1 (1971 Director William Friedkin)** Gene Hackman turning in a fine performance as mean but lovable 'Popeye' Doyle who relentlessly pursues drug traffickers and their boss 'Frog One'.

■ **One From The Heart (1983 Director Francis Ford Coppola)** Wonderful studio shot musical. A modern day *Singin' in the Rain* with great performances from Nastassja Kinski, the ever underrated Teri Garr and Frederick Forrest.

■ **San Francisco (1936 Director W.S. Van Dyke)** Clark Gable as cool barbary coast saloon owner in 1906 earthquake. Great special effects (last ten minutes) for a movie of this period.

■ **The Draughtsman's Contract (1982 Director Peter Greenaway)** Unusual stylized puzzle film as a draughtsman enters into an unusual (sexual) contract, for the

MEDIUM COOL
LITERATURE

Like music and the movies, literature is a great source of cool stimulus. Mr. and Miz Cool are both incredibly well read, highly selective, but anything but bookworms. They are keen followers of the lives and larger-than-life lifestyles of the cool authors, and occasionally have cool reveries of Paris in the Twenties when all the real bookmen were there – Hemingway, the Scott Fitzgeralds, Pound, Joyce, Beckett, and all those who hung out at the Hotel D'Angleterre, Silvia Beache's bookshop or Gertrude Stein's place at 28 Rue de Fleurus. Nowadays Coolits can be found hanging around London's Groucho Club.

In their homes you'll find the Cools' walls lined with countless rows of hard and paperback oeuvres of every colour, age, size and edition but which, like their classical record collection is forever chaotically incomplete. The Cools don't frequent libraries, they buy first edition and second hand.

The Cools can't make up their minds as to how much time they should allot to their reading. Whole piles of unread gems lie untouched by the side of their beds like uneaten hospital salads which are then swapped for another selection from time to time and equally ignored. Why should this be? Because it's important for the Cools to have the right books even if they don't necessarily read them. The Cools' library says as much about them as their record collection does. One random Harold Robbins between the Proust and the Balzac and it's curtains.

As well as a fertile source of ideas the Cools therefore use books as accessories. You see them on the tube or alone in the pub taking care to display cover and title for all to see. You won't find Cools devouring Mills and Boons, Barbara Cartlands, or 'Five Have It Off In Doncaster' anywhere in public. More likely a slim volume of Edgar Allan Poe. On their home turf the seemingly innocent Penguin modern classic left casually lying around is in fact as carefully arranged as a George Martin orchestration on a Beatles record, i.e. the book is meant to be discovered and admired without so much as a hint or prompt. 'Blimey, you're into this stuff are you? Really heavy' – 'What? Oh, that. Yes I enjoy a little light Goethe from time to time.'

Yet the Cools don't overdo their reading-posing. Unlike Sting who on the sleeve of *Synchronicity*, sits like a brooding Hamlet reading through spread fingers a copy of Jung. It's dubious cool since it's not at all obvious to anyone that the photographer, make-up artist, manicurist and hairdresser all just happened to be round while Mr. Sumner was undertaking a little literary digestion.

Of novels, it's difficult to say what makes for a cool read. A great story. A great sub-plot. A great style. Great characters. An awaken-

ing. A discovery. A catharsis. A fab ending. It's impossible to say. Cool novels are instinctively cool. You'll know one when you've read one. It doesn't have to be serious either. It could be as much a Fleming, a Chandler or a Wodehouse, as a Flaubert, Tolstoy or a Dickens.

Occasionally you'll hear a Cool say 'I don't read novels, only biographies'.

Occasionally you'll hear a Cool say 'I'm too busy writing to read anything'.

But that's only occasionally.

FIFTY SELECTED NOVELS
FROM THE COOL LIBRARY

■ **Dead Babies (1975) (retitled Dark Secrets) Martin Amis** The first literary nasty. Five characters in Appleseed Rectory spend a druggy weekend with a trio of Yanks. Someone called Johnny is out to destroy them. It's one of themselves.

■ **Gravity's Rainbow (1973) Thomas Pynchon** The war book to end them all – from the Howard Hughes of literary surrealists. It gives the impression that it contains the sum total of human knowledge up to now. Read also *V* and *The Crying of Lot 49* by the same author.

■ **The Magus (1966) John Fowles** A sleepy Greek island where Good and Evil is fought out against a constant parade of real and magical events. A man. A woman. Another woman. And then again. . . It's cool to read the revised edition next to the original to notice Fowles's changes, although the only real changes were more sex.

■ **The French Lieutenant's Woman (1969) John Fowles** Victorian England at its most revealing. Respectable engaged gentleman falls for fallen woman while the author takes a back seat as the characters escape from his control. He (the author) turns up two-thirds of the way through. Two endings to choose between.

■ **Devil in the Flesh (1923) Raymond Radiguet** Startling literary debut. Tragedy of a young teenage boy falling for an older married teenage chick. Boring it sounds. Boring it ain't.

■ **Froth on the Daydream (1947) Boris Vian** Surreal Daliesque tour de force. When the hero gives his friend money to get married, things go badly wrong.

■ **Against Nature (1884) Joris Karl Huysmans** Wilde said it was the strangest book he'd ever read. It recounts the exotic practices and perverse pleasures of a wealthy aesthete in search of an elusive ideal. A huge list of cool impedimenta.

■ **Doctor Faustus (1947) Thomas Mann** The genius of a composer and the horrifying price he has to pay for this achievement. True Cools will, however, read the original version – Goethe's *Faust*.

■ **Absolute Beginners (1959) Colin MacInnes** One part of the London Trilogy of novels. 'It was the tag-end of a London summer in the fifties and change simmered below the surface. . .' Teenagers. Pimps. Spades. Teds. Tarts. Coffee bars. Ah to have been there . . . forget the film . . . read the book.

■ **Slaughterhouse 5 (1969) Kurt Vonnegut** World War POW reality. Jumps in time. Aliens from another world. The wanderings of Billy Pilgrim in and out of everything. Fab ending.

■ **The Roads to Freedom (1945, 1947, 1949) Jean Paul Sartre** A trilogy. Paris 1938 through the war. Hero without scruples or morals learns the meaning of commitment.

■ **The Mosquito Coast (1981) Paul Theroux** Superbly composed. Clever and terrifying. Story of genius madman inventor who forsakes America and takes his family to start a new and idyllic life in Honduras. The dream turns into a nightmare.

■ **Le Grand Meaulnes (1912) Alain-Fournier** 'The Wanderer'. One of the great French novels of the century and the only one by its author who died in WW1. The twilight world between boyhood and manhood. Mystical.

■ **Les Enfants Terribles (1929) Jean Cocteau** The children of the game. A brother and sister must die in following out the rules of the 'game' which they invented as their own eccentric version of life itself.

■ **Titus Groan, (1946) Gormenghast (1950) Mervyn Peake** A gothic fantasy. A great castle. Gor-

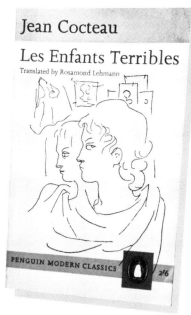

Jean Cocteau
Les Enfants Terribles
Translated by Rosamond Lehmann
PENGUIN MODERN CLASSICS 2/6

menghast and its labyrinthian passages, rooms and characters. Titus inherits the throne of a dynasty based on bureaucratic order. Ambitious kitchen-hand Steerpike defies the immemorial order and goes on an orgy of violence and destruction. A totally original creation. Gordon Sumner's favourite book. He's already secured the film rights. NB *Titus Alone* (1959) the third book in the trilogy was written when the author was mentally ill and consequently reflects his condition but not the greatness of the first two books.

■ **The Catcher in the Rye (1951) J.D. Salinger** A key work of the Fifties. The youthful hero who rebels but as a gentle voice of protest. F-funny. F-sad. F-classic.

■ **The Great Gatsby (1926) F. Scott Fitzgerald** The genius jazz age writer who invented a generation. A fabulously rich unknown impresses the world with his mulah but fails to score points with his old girlfriend. The light on Daisy's dock is the eternal image of what you can never have. The last sentence 'So we beat on, boats against the current, borne back ceaselessly into the past', is truly heavy *merde* indeed.

■ **Ulysses (1922) James Joyce** The coolest book to name drop in crowded wine bars even if you haven't read it. Long difficult assimilation of classical myth and history into the events of one day in Dublin in 1904. One of the greatest novels of the century. Brilliant parodies of styles from Anglo-Saxon brutalism to *Bunty* magazine.

■ **Catch 22 (1961) Joseph Heller** Life on USAF base on a Med. Island in WW2. A series of brilliant funny vignettes of the people behind uniforms. Everything tends towards madness as the only 'reason' behind human activity. Satire of the first order.

■ **Vathek (1786) William Beckford** A classic of gothic fiction in which the Caliph Vathek – a servant of the Devil – possesses the power to kill with a glance, and after venturing to the ruined city of Ista-

COOL

A N

ARABIAN TALE,

FROM AN

UNPUBLISHED MANUSCRIPT:

WITH

N O T E S

CRITICAL AND EXPLANATORY.

LONDON:

Printed for J. JOHNSON, in ST. PAUL'S CHURCH-YARD,

AND ENTERED AT THE STATIONERS' HALL.

MDCCLXXXVI.

Vathek. Pre-figures all the Hammer Studio's output by 200 years

kar, dies of an exploding heart. The novel was written at a single sitting lasting forty-eight hours. It prefigures all the Hammer studio output by two hundred years.

■ **On the Road (1957) Jack Kerouac** The Lonesome Voyager as mythmaker. This bible of the Beat Generation follows the wanderings, pick-ups, dope trips, jazz junkets and endless movement across America of Sal Paradise (Kerouac) and Dean Moriarty (Neal Cassady) in a style that mingles a stream of consciousness fluency with bursts of astonishing rhapsody.

■ **Lolita (1955) Vladimir Nabokov** A rapture of illicit love. European stuffed shirt writer falls for twelve-year-old nymphet and with her is pursued across America. A masterpiece of coolly perfect style, exact description and swooning prose – the Rockies are 'heart- and sky-piercing snow-veined colossi of stone'...

■ **Tristram Shandy (1759) Laurence Sterne** A unique, bawdy, formless, anarchic, good-natured dig at the Age of Reason, couched as a biography that can't keep up with its subject's real life.

■ **The Serial (1976) Cyra McFadden** The classic textbook of Californian psychobabble, where everyone mellows out, gets behind things like

Vladimir Nabokov

ironing boards and generally interacts all over the place.

■ **By Grand Central Station I Sat Down and Wept (1966) Elizabeth Smart** Short, unforgettable prose poem of lost love, densely written and not easy to penetrate. Intensely moving (Cools can be moved). Unlike any other.

■ **Other Voices. Other Rooms. (1945) Truman Capote** When Joel Knox's mother dies, he is sent into the exotic unknown of the Deep South to live with a father he has never seen. But everyone is curiously evasive when Joel asks to see his father. First novel. A brilliant, searching study of homosexuality set in a shimmering land-

scape of heat, mystery and decadence.

■ **The Razor's Edge (1944) W. Somerset Maugham** Having written *Of Human Bondage* (1915) and *Cakes and Ale* (1930) R.E. was published at the age of seventy. The main character, Larry, lives on the Razor's Edge in his search for *the way*, ie the meaning of life, etc. A moving and enlightened study of human desires, agonies and triumphs.

■ **A Clockwork Orange (1962) Anthony Burgess** The cult of ultra-violence expounded long before the football-terrorist violence of the Seventies and Eighties. Burgess is a literary genius who writes exceedingly well. Later filmed by Kubrick, this one even invented its own vocabulary.

■ **The Old Man and the Sea (1952) Ernest Hemingway** An old Cuban fisherman goes out with his boat and sights a great marlin. Like a matador with a bull, he feels drawn to the magnificent creature, so that, though one has to kill the other, he does not mind who kills whom. Full of allegorical flourishes.

■ **The Tin Drum (1959) Gunter Grass** Certainly the strangest, probably the greatest novel to come out of Germany in years. A little boy nevers grows up but shrewdly

observes the coming of totalitarianism. Lots of sex. Lots of eels.

■ **East of Eden (1952) John Steinbeck** Two brothers, one woman, two sons. Cain and Abel. A Californian epic of innocence and experience, good and evil. Later filmed very thinly with James Dean in the role of the well meaning Cain.

■ **Darkness at Noon (1940) Arthur Koestler** A grimly fascinating interpretation of the logic of the Russian Revolution, as an old Bolshevik awaits death in prison.

■ **The Outsider (1942) Albert Camus** Once again, Camus indulges in his favourite subject – the absurdity of life. Beautiful simple story of a man wrongly accused of murder but who faces execution because he can't be bothered to defend himself.

■ **Brideshead Revisited (1945) Evelyn Waugh** Charles, Sebastian, pre-war Oxford and Venice, Brideshead Castle. The upper class in decline. You've seen the TV series now read the book.

■ **The Trial (1925) Franz Kafka** A man arrested on a charge that is never specified. The story is a *Pilgrims' Progress* of the subconscious. A nightmare of non-logic where reality is entangled with imagination.

■ **The Long Goodbye (1953) Raymond Chandler** For cool reading read lots and lots of Chandler. His Philip Marlowe is as immortal as Sherlock Holmes. Another complicated Southern Californian murder mystery where cynical Marlowe for once experiences the pangs of friendship.

■ **Brave New World (1932) Aldous Huxley** Life in the future. A witty and biting satire of scientific progress, which predicted amongst other things test-tube babies and 'feelies'. Probably the author's most popular.

■ **Point Counter Point (1928) Aldous Huxley** A great fantasia of extraordinary people and profound ideas. Intellectuals, aristocratic debutantes abound in the disrupted English society of the Twenties. Laughter gives way to mysticism which later engulfed the author.

■ **Do Androids Dream of Electric Sheep (1968) Philip K. Dick** Cult status Science Fiction novelist. David Pringle's *SF The 100 Best Novels* lists six of Dick's. *Androids* is the book on which *Blade Runner* was based. Can an android be human? If so, why can't he be treated as such?

■ **At Swim 2 Birds (1939) Flann O'Brien** An Irish student, who when not lying in bed or pub crawling, is writing about a man named Trellis who is writing a book about his enemies, who in revenge are writing a book about him. Brilliant deconstruction of the assumptions that lie behind fiction-making.

■ **The World According to Garp (1976) John Irving** Women's Lib or rather Men's Lib. Garp's mum decides she never wants to have anything to do with men, but first she must have a son. She makes love once to a dying serviceman in hospital who unknowingly grants her wish before he dies. Great book, great themes; family, love, loyalty, individuality, rape, middle-American way of life.

■ **The Unlimited Dream Company (1979) J.G. Ballard** A man steals a plane, crash lands and either experiencing death and afterlife, or renewed life, he becomes Messiah to a group who see him as a redeemer.

■ **1984 (1949) George Orwell** A terrifying version of the future which seems to have passed us by. Today the nearest things to big brother seem to be quiz shows, the Inland Revenue, insurance men, the phone company (see the film *Winter Kills*) and Ariel boil wash commercials.

■ **The History Man (1975) Malcolm Bradbury** Howard Kirk, lecturer in sociology – a radical so long as the same privileges are disallowed to elements he calls 'reactionary'. The university campus. The new permissiveness. Sit-ins. Habitat furniture. European History essays disguised as political tracts. Set in the Sixties, a perfect evocation of crappy, bogus ideology.

■ **Nostromo (1904) Joseph Conrad** Conrad's best book. As an ambitious feat of imagination it has been compared to *War and Peace*. Amid the grandiose scenery of South America, against the exciting events of a revolution, men are ironically displayed not as isolated beings, but as social animals.

■ **Bright Lights, Big City (1984) Jay McInery** A chronicle of hedonistic New York night life. The story of an educated, middle-class young man, working in a humble capacity on a highly reputable literary magazine, dreaming of becoming a great writer, yet squandering his talent and energies in a desperate cycle of coke-sniffing and night-clubbing. A morality tale with a happy ending.

■ **The Spire (1964) William Golding** The addition of a spire to a cathedral involves the commission of more acts of evil than seems proper for an innocent human undertaking.

■ **A Confederacy of Dunces (1980) John Kennedy Toole** A sad history to the book. The author committed suicide after it was rejected by everyone for publication. Later it was awarded a posthumous Pulitzer Prize. The eccentric hero believing his real home to be in the Middle Ages, revolts against the modern world in New Orleans, with savagely comic results.

■ **Steppenwolf (1927) Herman Hesse** Hesse is one of those strange authors like Vonnegut, Scott Fitzgerald and Huxley who are better read in your late teens/ early twenties. The Steppenwolf is a Faust-like and magical story of the humanization of a middle-aged misanthrope.

■ **Alice in Wonderland (1865) Lewis Carroll** A phantasmagorical unrepeatable tale which like Smarties, *Tis Was* and *The Jungle Book*, is enjoyed equally by adults, supposedly for more aesthetic reasons. In a dream Alice pursues a white rabbit underground and enters a world where she meets fantastic creatures. A classic of surrealism.

ELEVEN COOL POETS

John Donne Because of his way with women, death and God. Because of his little Ronald Coleman moustache.

William Blake Because he saw angels looking at him through the window. Because he once asked his wife if she'd mind if he screwed the maid.

Thomas Chatterton Because he killed himself in despair of ever being recognised, published, feted or paid. He was eighteen.

George Gordon, Lord Byron Because in spite of a club foot, he made everyone fall in love with him. Because he fought for freedom in Greece. Because his Don Juan has the wittiest rhymes in the whole of English poetry.

John Wilmot, Earl of Rochester Because he was a cavalier's son, a soldier, a hell-raiser and theologian who wrote very rude poems about genitalia and sanitary wear and died young at thirty-three.

Samuel Taylor Coleridge Because he was the last man to have read absolutely everything ever written (you can't do it today unless you're Dr. Jonathan Miller or Bernard Levin). Because he let opium prevent his brilliant brain from ever finishing anything except Kubla Kahn.

Algernon Swinburne Because of his shameless, self-confessed love for sexual agony and large women with whips.

Rupert Brooke Because he was such an enthusiast. Even patriots

can be cool sometimes. Because he wrote 'We shall go down with unrepentant tread/rose-crowned into the darkness'.

Robert Lowell Because he was so intensely brilliant his brain went into constant overdrive (he referred to his madness as 'speeding up'). Because he wrote *For the Union Dead*.

Thom Gunn Because of his leather jacket (a poet in a leather jacket? Yup.)

Robert Graves Because he was unique. He followed no fads and set no fashions. He had a mind like an alchemist's laboratory – everything that got into it came out new, weird and gleaming. Because he got into the *Times* obituary column twice (1916) and (1985).

COOL MAGAZINES/NEWSPAPERS
TO BE SEEN WITH OR
TO LEAVE CASUALLY LYING
ROUND THE HOUSE

- *French Vogue* – on import £5.40.
- *The Face.*
- *Tatler.*
- *Le Monde.*
- *The New York Times.*
- *Private Eye.*
- *Heavy Metal (Metal Hurlant).*
- *Ritz.*
- *Maledicta* (the international journal of verbal aggression).
- *Select.*
- *Creative Review.*
- *Books and Bookmen.*
- *Zoom.*
- *Nova* (Sixties fashion magazine).

UNCOOL RAGS

- *Amateur Photographer.*
- *The Sporting Times.*
- *The Daily Star.*
- Stacks of Sunday colour supplements.
- *Investors' Chronicle.*
- Yesterday's papers.
- *Computer magazines.*
- *LAM.*
- *9 to 5.*
- *Portrait.*
- *Socialist Worker.*
- *Zipper.*
- *Hustler.*
- *Hot Rod.*
- *I.d.*
- *Rolling Stone.*

UNCOOL LITERATURE

Harold Robbins 'After sixty-seven hours of continuous and depraved love making amongst the deafening roar of several Ferrari V12 Formula One engines that echoed from countless banks of loudspeakers around the bedroom Stella Starlet was amazed to discover Storm still hadn't come'.

Thomas Covenanters Despite being a complete and abject failure in his own time and country, the hero suddenly discovers himself to be a powerful figure in the 'Nice Land' where he becomes the sole hope that keeps a beautiful blonde aristocratic race from imminent destruction at the hands of evil wart-covered wargs.

Stephen King/Sidney Sheldon Get a beautiful and sensuous temptress with fanged teeth and pert breasts to smile from the cover. Once we've sold fifty thousand copies of that we'll get a computer to write the book.

Dennis Wheatley Black magic. Goats. Ghost hunters. Hitler reincarnated. Four thousand pages a time.

Jackie Collins Geriatric (ie anyone over fifty) movie people discover true happiness after fucking everyone in the world and then discovering it was their original teenage love they only ever wanted in the first place.

Tom Sharpe books People crying with laughter on crowded tube trains. 'His other ones are even funnier.' 'What about that one with the blow-up doll.' 'Did you see Blot on the telly? A scream wasn't it?'

Scantily dressed tarts on the cover books With titles like *The Power Broker*, *The International Banker*, *The Onanist*, etc.

Vet Books 'So different from the TV series, and yet so like it, didn't you find?'

Fart and bum books.

Books on willies or wallies.

Books on mysticism, etc. Astral travelling, numerology, Zen and art of washing machine maintenance, self-actualization, self-realization, love signs, star signs, fortune telling by runes, fortune telling by skinheads.

Encyclopaedias Ersatz-leather bound cheap volumes of twelve just to fill space in the library and give an impression of higher learning.

Book of the Month Club Limited edition. Gold-leaf encrusted. Embroidered offerings of rare qual-

ity and distinction. 'Amazing first time offer of 17p for the complete works of Dickens.'

MEDIUM COOL
TV

> *'Television is for appearing on, not looking at.'*
> (NOEL COWARD)

If you absolutely must, and you can't do as Howard Beale/Peter Finch advocated in *Network*, ie throw your TV sets out the window (how come only Keith Richards and Keith Moon ever listened?) then like most Cools you have several TVs, one for the bedroom being an absolute necessity, even though you rarely watch them.

The Cools used to enjoy appearing on the Michael Parkinson Chat Show, nowadays they wouldn't be seen dead on Terry Wogan's or Joan Rivers'. Much of their time is spent watching *Question Time*, the News from every channel, *Greavsie and Saint*, *40 minutes*, repeats of *Lou Grant* and *Hill Street Blues*. They always tape *The World About Us*, and similar nature programmes but never have time to watch them. The Cools appreciate Tony Hancock but don't want to broadcast that fact too loudly and widely since *Private Eye* once mercilessly caricatured the Hancock aficiando in their *Great Bores of Today* section.

First and foremost, every Cool is familiar with the following TV dialogue, taken from *The Prisoner*:

Q *Where am I?*
A In the Village.
Q *What do you want?*
A Information.
Q *Whose side are you on?*
A That would be telling. We want information . . . information . . . information.
Q *You won't get it!*
A By hook or by crook, we will.
Q *Who are you?*
A The new number two.
Q *Who is number one?*
A You are number six.
Q *I am not a number, I am a free man.*
A Ha, Ha, Ha, Ha, Ha, Ha, Ha, Ha.

The Cools have every one of the thirteen episodes on tape. They know the plots backwards, and fundamentally disagree with the almost universally held opinion of the cop-out ending in the final episode. The Cools understand what McGoohan was trying to say just as they understood *2001 A Space Odyssey* without having to refer to Arthur C. Clarke's book for guidance.

The Cools' favourite bit of dialogue from *The Prisoner (above right)* crops up from time to time in the series usually in flashback. Their ambition is to use it one day in a conflict situation, eg with a bank manager, an employer, a supermarket checkout girl.

With these words, McGoohan ensures forever his place in the cool catalogue.

A quick glance through the Cools' video collection will reveal some of the following ☞

A selection of *Sergeant Bilko* (thirty or forty episodes). The funniest, and fastest, series ever made for TV. Bilko has always been an endearing character (not hero) to the Cools and he will be sadly missed.

The original Max Headroom pilot. Cool Couple – Edison Carter (Matt Frewer) and Dominique (Hilary Tindall).

Early *Doctor Who* episodes – currently going down a storm in the US of A on late night TV. Early doctors being William Hartnell, Patrick Troughton and Jon Pertwee.

A selection of *Saturday Night Live* (the American series with John Belushi, Dan Ackroyd, Steve Martin, Lily Tomlin, etc.).

The *Edge of Darkness* TV series. Cool couple – Joe Don Baker/Bob Peck foil evil nuclear waste scheme.

The *Dead Head* TV series. A modern Jack the Ripper conspiracy shot on video with cool slob central character Denis Lawson.

Bewitched. The lovely witch housewife married to the long suffering ad agent.

Ready, Steady, Go! The weekend starts here. Mod parties every Friday night.

I, Claudius.

Selected *Young Ones* (The Party. The Bomb.)

Danger Man (Cool Patrick McG once again).

The Outer Limits.

Black Adder 2.

Clive James's interview with Roman Polanski over dinner in his Parisian apartment. Polanski, a master of cool, side-stepping leading questions into his private life giving straight but enigmatic answers. See Clive James squirm.

Auf Weidersehen Pet. First series.

Blind Date.

Miami Vice.

The complete Sean Connery/James Bond movie collection.

The first three episodes of *Brideshead Revisited* – for Oxford as it was – Sebastian throwing up into Charles's room and the high-camp exhortations of Anthony B-B-Blanche (Nicholas Grace).

The Avengers. Clean cool Steed (Patrick MacNee). Clean cool Emma Peal, Diana Rigg, Swinging

Sixties London kinkiness. A Bentley 4½ litre. A Lotus Elan S2. Beautiful apartments. Civil servants wanting to take over the world. Plenty of James Bond-like smart-alec quips.

UNCOOL TV

Game for a Laugh (Probably the greatest embarrassment of all time, not counting Bernard Manning's appearance on *The Joan Rivers Show*). The Cools recall with fond remembrance a *Not the Nine O'Clock News* pastiche when Rowan Atkinson returns home to find his wife's head has been cut off and then realizes he's on *Game for a Laugh*: 'You mean you guys cut her head off? What a bunch of loonies. Just wait till I tell the wife . . .' Shriek as if in pain. Squawk like buzzards.

The Price is Right What else do you do with a man who has appeared in Stork commercials?

Fat, tall, short, thin comedian double acts on early Saturday evening '. . . and of course it turns out to be the mother in law!' Shriek as if in pain. Squawk like buzzards.

International Darts 'And all this fat beer-swilling bastard needs is a double 19 . . . and he's got it . . . but the cameraman missed it. . .'

The Muppets Dated cool.

Grandstand Especially a six hour session that takes in wrestling and horse racing.

Match of the Day 'That leaves them three points clear at the top of the table Jimmy.'

The Big Match 'That leaves them three points clear at the top of the table Brian.'

Terry Wogan 'Terry you're such a scream, even though no one's ever heard of you in America.'

Brookside 'Well I had to have an affair with his wife, I was so depressed. I mean I was unemployed even before I was born.'

That's Life 'So we visited Mr. Armstrong of Ripley only to find he'd been dead for eight years . . . Cyril?' 'Yes Esther. I had composed a poem about poor Mrs Clark's lost savings but I left it at home in the lavatory.' Laugh like a hyena on Panama Red.

Cheap video sitcoms with out of control laugh/applause machines from the U.S. of A 'You mean she walked out on you?' (mild laughter) 'Yup, and now I'm gonna commit suicide!' (roars of laughter).

Treasure Hunt 'Anneka you must've run 4,119 miles and yet you don't seem to have shaken off any excess ballast.'

That's Life (Cont.) '. . . So then we visited Mr Aziz at his London home but he told Cyril to fuck off.'

Bonanza Fat Sunday lunch. Fat background noise. Fat sleep. Fat studio-bound TV rerun chronicling the adventures of Fat actors. ZZZZZ.

And many, many more.

MEDIUM COOL
ART

'Comment still to come'

(ANON)

Since no one has ever been able to agree on one definition of art [there are many brilliant: *'The aim of art is to represent not the outward appearance of things, but their inner significance'* (Aristotle) as well as pretentious *'Every work of art is a child of its time'* (Wassily Kandinsky) definitions], it is difficult to say what makes for cool painting and painters, sculptures and sculptors, etc.

Generally the Cools appreciate that in essence all art is cool so long as it is produced with the right creative intention: ie 'I feel a passionate need to produce this' rather than 'This piece of junk's gonna make me a million bucks'.

All artists are cool in the Cools' book, especially when they're in their own environment, ie they may be a real bore outside the studio but in it they mesmerise.

Most con-artists are cool (ie fakers of art) – eg Tom Keating who successfully reproduced (ie faked) Samuel Palmers to the terminal

embarrassment of the art world, and those buyers who couldn't tell a real Samuel Palmer from a toilet brush. The crazy thing is that the art world is so screwy Tom Keating fakes are now actually big money in their own right.

Needless to say, the so called 'art world' is generally considered to be uncool.

The auction houses who set the prices and the so called 'purchasers' of art whose only real cultural achievement is the ability to sign cheques for huge amounts of money – 'I paid £8 million for this early Rembrandt, so it must be good'. Doubtless in a couple of years time it'll be sold unknowingly back to the same person for £12 million, and so on. In fact, most famous collections wind up in lead-lined vaults where no one can see them. So why bother.

Cool people enjoy art and will talk about it till it's time to go out to dinner. They don't see *art* as an investment.

COOL THINGS TO SAY
ABOUT ART IN A GALLERY

- That's a nice painting.
- I don't like that at all. It's horseshit.
- That's a firebucket actually, not a Henry Moore.
- The best thing about Chagall is his signature.

■ Nice tits in those days.
■ Whoever heard of a blue period?
■ Pretty colours don't you think?
■ How come he didn't finish the sky?
■ It's well known that the splodgy bit in the corner was actually the result of a heavy cold.
■ It would look much better upside down, as the artist originally intended.
■ Is that a Brick or a Braque? (Chortle Chortle).
■ Bacon must've had a few when he painted that.
■ I'd buy it but it's too big for my living room.
■ Of course it's a fake. I own the original.
■ Well it makes no impression on me.

COOL THINGS TO DO IN AN ART GALLERY

■ Pick somebody up.
■ Read the *Beano*.
■ Examine a painting close-up with a magnifying glass and nod knowingly.

UNCOOL THINGS TO SAY ABOUT ART IN A GALLERY

■ Such exquisite brush work.
■ It evokes his childhood totally.
■ Such passion for one so unpassionate. Such sensitivity for one so insensitive.

- Cubism was a valid reaction to the Civil War of course.
- Mad of course. But brilliant.
- Of course, he couldn't make up his mind whether he was post-modernist or Pre-Raphaelite. The results are all too obvious.
- He never sold a painting in his lifetime you know . . . (yawn).
- Such wit. Such gaiety. And yet such repression.
- The structure is all wrong but it works surprisingly well.
- He demonstrates the insight of a Matisse but the discipline of a Vermeer.
- It says everything there is to say about art (ie bugger all).

UNCOOL THINGS TO DO IN AN ART GALLERY

- Stand about discussing a piece of work in a stilted intellectual manner, blocking everyone's view of the painting and drawing attention to yourself.
- View pictures from at least six feet away with crossed arms while leaning on your back foot.
- Stare at the same picture for ages as if there's nothing else in the gallery that could remotely interest you.
- Walk the wrong way round to everyone else.
- Break wind.
- Flash.
- Have an anxiety attack.

There's not much more the Cools need to know about art except what they like and the odd good Salvador Dali story.

THE SALVADOR DALI STORY

There's a Salvador Dali story that dates back to the Fifties. The great man has been commissioned by Max Factor, the cosmetics house, to design the brand identity and

packaging of a new fragrance. Dali says OK, but give me a free hand and complete secrecy, and don't bug me with requests for sneak previews. Max Factor agree. The big day finally arrives. The world's press are there. Dali arrives in great pomp and ceremony but immediately causes concern because he's got nothing under his arm, not even a layout pad. The cameras are flashing like crazy. Dali approaches the stage. Just before he gets there he bends down, picks up a hot discarded flash bulb from one of those old fashioned press cameras and resumes his journey to the podium. The audience falls into a hushed silence. 'Ladies and gentlemen of the press' he exclaims with a flourish 'I give you . . .' and then he holds up the discarded flash bulb he's picked up just thirty seconds ago . . . 'Electrique!' The press go ape with excitement, Max Factor breath a sigh of relief and needless to say the brand becomes one of the most popular and enduring in the Max Factor range.

Need one say more?

COOL PHOTO

Check out the following if you haven't already done so.

Robert Mapplethorpe Heavy gay macho street gang violence pix. The current favourite of the New York set.

COOL

Lee Miller Stunningly beautiful model and mistress of Man Ray. Friend of many including Picasso and Ghandi. Wife of Sir Roland Penrose. A war photographer who was always in the right place at the right time.

Diane Arbus The psychic nightmares behind the Sixties American dream. A tragic private life leading to her suicide in 1971. How much was her work the product or the cause of her mental state?

Bruce Weber Black and white, girls and boys with athletic bodies in a variety of Fifties classic poses. The Calvin Klein sex and beefcake look.

Bill Brandt Heartbreakingly simple black and white images full of form, shade and light. Nature. Poverty. Families. Industry.

May Ray More artist than photographer. *The* influence on everyone. Surrealist Daliesque pictures. Brandt was his assistant at one time.

John Deacon Forgotten Sixties photographer. Mainly portraits. Recently rediscovered.

Henri Cartier Bresson Possibly the best for reportage. Great chronicler of French way of life, his little Leica forever at the ready.

Not to mention all that wonderful work by Cecil Beaton, Karsh of Ottowa, Norman Parkinson, the Bailey Brigade, Jeanloup Sieff, Don McCullin, Guy Bourdin, Helmut Newton, Angus McBean, J.H. Lartigue, Horst, Penn, Avedon, Stern, Steichen, Snowdon, Sarah Moon, Kertesz and Ansel Adams.

Avoid for uncool: David Hamilton, the guy who soft photographs underage girls in a variety of clinches with white doves flying around. 'I was just washing Ann-Marie's hair when her singlet fell open and her breasts were invitingly revealed'. And avoid all those photographers who claim in an *Amateur Photographer* kind of way that 'you too can photograph a nude like this after only three or four lessons'.

Avoid Patrick Lichfield's world's most beautiful women collections and Unipart calendars.

NB: Pirelli Calendars were re-introduced in 1984 after a ten year absence and due to their limited availability are very collectable.

Sport is a great source of cool, but it raises somewhat of a dilemma since it is usually limited to the field, the track or the pitch or in the stadium, etc. but rarely afterwards.

On the track, Seb Coe is the king of calculated cool as he runs a crucial race, coming from nowhere and breaking records with the frequency of an out-of-control jukebox. Yet, the moment he steps into his smart C&A casuals, he loses a lot of cool credibility.

Footballers too have their moments. It was cool to win the World Cup in 1966, especially beating the Jerries for the first time since 1945. But interviewed back in the changing rooms or back in the studio, it's usually straight back to the old 'back of the net Brian' – 'where did you get your perm?' – syndrome.

No one was cooler than George Best in his heyday (rubbing his boots on the opposition's goalposts after he'd scored a goal). No one's cooler than Ian Botham on a good day. But as the Cools know only too well, you have to be cool in your private life as well as your public one.

As games go, the Cools are particularly partial to cricket. Plenty of sunny summer pitches in sleepy olde English villages. Plenty of posing, plenty of Pimms and pints. Best of all, there's always the lucky swing or spinner which will either turn an almost definite duck

into a confident boundary, or a wide into a wicket. The spectators applaud with amazement. You, on the other hand, take it all in your confident stride.

Mr. Cool hates body building on the Schwarzenegger scale and would rather play football and rugby occasionally and purely for enjoyment. Miz Cool hates jolly hockey sticks and so confines herself to working-out, dance, jazz etc. Both Cools have a fairly relaxed and open attitude towards jogging and running so long as the weather's warm (which it rarely is so you don't have to go out that often) and both are keen tennis players. Mr. Cool dabbles with squash while Miz Cool is a demon badminton player.

For both, sport is more for pure enjoyment than for health and competitive spirit, although neither intend to lose to anyone, ever.

Hang gliding Once is enough. Twice is suicidal – 'Sure I've done hang gliding. Hasn't everybody?'

Gliding Very Steve McQueen. Very *Thomas Crown Affair*. You can almost hear the *Windmills of your Mind* when you're gliding.

Rock climbing As cool and dangerous as hang gliding. (cf the TV climbs of Don Whillans and Joe Brown). In a dangerous situation the thing to do is roll a cigarette and smoke it until the solution becomes obvious. Needless to say there are a lot of chain smokers in this sport.

Pot holing/caving Very elitist. Very European. Very dangerous. Plenty of *cool* camaraderie.

Parachuting Once is quite enough. Remember to rub the boot-mark off your bum before you re-enter the clubhouse.

Sailing On big ocean-going bastards with at least three masts. Not in spacky little dinghies with names like 'Ahoy there' that float around on Golden Ponds in Chichester Harbour.

Surfing The lone blond wolves of the Dennis Wilson variety. Catch a wave and you're sitting on top of the world. Miss it and you go scuba diving without an oxygen tank.

Windsurfing On wild stormy coastal waters not in sheltered Greek Island Bays. Standing up from the water line and all that stuff.

Fishing In sleepy English rivers. Or the Hemingway way: Levi rivets and stitching at full stretch as you go for the big marlin in Florida waters. (Of course Cools always let the fish go afterwards.)

Polo Stewart Copeland. Charles Windsor. Thomas Crown. Fergie's

dad. The cool sport for the relatively astronomically rich.

Gas ballooning Like buying a Concorde ticket to nowhere. Up in the air for two hours then you let £500 worth of helium out.

UNCOOL SPORTS

Stockcar racing Eel pie and mash while you watch a Demolition Derby. Although it's very satisfying to see all those Datsuns being smashed about, there's never a Volvo in sight.

Cockfighting / bull fighting / fox hunting Bloodsports are uncool period.

Greyhound racing Hardly Kelly's idea of a great night out, but you never know.

Boxing Look what it did to Henry Cooper, Cassius Clay, Frank Bruno, etc.

Horse racing Apart from Ascot, the Cools find that horse racing has all the intrigue of a Fassbinder film without sub-titles.

Motor racing Yawn. Not like in the good old days of Fangio and Jim Clark. Nowadays it's all about engines and pit teams, not drivers. The real glamour of the sport has virtually disappeared.

Rugby league He may be a big lad who can take a bit of slap and tickle in the showers, but that's as far as it goes.

Golf If they didn't wear such silly trousers it might be OK. But they do, so it isn't.

Bowls Grannie/grandad cool.

Swimming at public baths Bald heads. Fearsome goggles. Chlorine. Suffocation. The resounding cheer of schoolkids. No ta. Synchronized swimming is particularly uncool. Private pools and oceans are the only places to swim.

COOL PASTIMES

Ten pin bowling Bowling shirts and sneakers. Teenage *Back to the Future cool.*

Backgammon Omar and me at Aspinall's. He may have won but I got to meet Stephanie of Monaco.

Chess East bloc intellectual cool.

Bridge West bloc intellectual cool.

Baccarat 'Bond curled his right hand in, glanced briefly down and flipped the cards face up into the middle of the table. "Le neuf", said the croupier.' (*Casino Royale*)

Poker One of the greatest games of

cool. Draw or stud it doesn't matter. Marathon matches (ten hours or more) are the best and it helps if it's daytime when you open the blinds. Easy on the Jim Beam. Hard on the raising.

Snooker At home or in a private club. *Not* on telly.

Softball Up and coming summer casual cool.

Waterskiing Preferably on one ski rather than two. But whichever you choose, avoid the big beach finish. It's uncool to do it brilliantly. It's uncool to end up with a trunk full of sand.

Gardening Relaxed mindless back to nature cool. Mr. Cool is as much of an enthusiast as Miz Cool and vice versa.

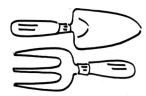

Trivial Pursuit Verging on questionable cool since you can never answer a question when it's your turn, but you can always answer everyone else's.

UNCOOL PASTIMES

Playing space invader machines

in amusement arcades Next to Wimpy Bars there is nowhere less cool than an amusement arcade, especially ones with highly original titles like 'Lots-O-Fun'.

Betting on horses in a betting shop Next to amusement arcades there's nowhere less cool than a betting shop, not even Woolworths.

Going to the sales The Cools never go to the sales. Too degrading.

Seances 'Can you tell me if Uncle Desmond's there? Yes or no. Uncle Desmond? Where exactly did your wife leave her car keys?'

Pool Poor man's snooker.

Knitting Embroidery is OK, but knitting is about as interesting as watching paint dry.

Queuing For Springsteen or *Out of Africa* tickets. For Wimbledon or the bus. **The Cools never, never, never queue.** Not even for peanut butter and caviare sandwiches in Leningrad.

Washing the Car Especially on a Sunday when everyone in Acacia Avenue is also doing the same thing. Worse still if you spend hours touching up rust spots. What's a car-wash for, f'crissakes?

Outdoor Graffiti Gone are the days when grafitti amused ('*Renew his interests in carpentry. Saw his head off*'). All we get now is several thousand permutations of 'Chelsea/WHUC/Tottenham/Arsenal/QPR are not very talented, OK!'

D.I.Y. The very initials strike terror into the hearts of the Cools, and conjure up nightmare visions of trips to Texas, B&Q and other homecare branches where all the happy families go.

Strolling over commons and parks with a metal detector Discover hidden caches of ½p bits buried by the Bank of England, useless cooking utensils from forgotten camping trips, and old unexploded WW2 bombs.

Baking your own bread Apparently you can buy it in the shops, it's much cheaper and it doesn't take hours to make.

Doing the quick crossword Mindless relaxation, and everyone knows that another word for 'look' is 'see'.

Watching the colour testcard Don't laugh, some people do.

Home brewing Sprout and mashed swede wine. Foaming pints of soapy bitter that costs 7p a pint. So why pay more? I'll tell you why – because I want to live for a while.

P O I N T   O N E

Making sure of your audience
Despite all your efforts, at the end
of the day it's your audience who
decides whether you're cool or not.

You may temporarily fool
yourself when you play your cricket-
bat guitar to the strains of Shadows
tracks in front of your bedroom
mirror, but sooner or later, you'll
realize you've got to get out there
and strut your stuff.

P O I N T   T W O

**Being uncool is far worse than
not being cool** There is nothing
worse than the aspiring young cool
blade who gets it totally wrong. To
be uncool, to commit an uncool
crime is eleven times worse than
not quite achieving cool status.

There are small uncool faux
pas you can just about get away
with, eg a diamond in the tooth or a
hidden tattoo. There are big uncool
faux pas you just can't hide, eg
owning a Volvo or reading Jonathan
Livingstone Seagull.

P O I N T   T H R E E

**'The Michael J. Pollard syn-
drome'** Anyone anywhere can be
cool. In the film *Little Fauss. Big
Halsy* hunky Robert Redford is the
ace cool motorcycle racer who gets
all the chicks. Small squirt Pollard
is the mechanic who gets nowt but

a lot of unpaid overtime. Their
fortunes turn full circle. Pollard
becomes a better racer and so
becomes the Big man of the track.
[**Conclusion.** It's not what you look
like it's what you do and how you
act.]

P O I N T   F O U R

**You can lose it as quickly as you
got it, and vice versa** The Clash
had it instantly then lost it completely by farting around the hip US
coke snorting/tuxedo wearing set
and losing all their social conscien-
ce. Similar cool withdrawals hap-
pend to Johnnie Rotten, Kenny
Everett and Simon Dee. Tony Black-
burn, on the other hand, was a prat
of the first order in his Radio 1 days,
but after twenty years finally
achieved near-cucumber status as
Britain's longest and best promoter
of black music.

P O I N T   F I V E

**If you can't cut it in your own
back yard don't despair** Just because you can't set their souls
alight in Streatham or you weren't
born to run in Bradford doesn't
mean there's no hope for you in the
outside world. Lawrence Durrell,
Henry Miller, Jimmie Hendrix,
Dylan Thomas and Karl Marx all
made their marks elsewhere. Sometimes you just need a change of
scene from your home turf.

P O I N T   S E V E N

From West to East Cultural influences are shifting away from America back to Europe and back to the East. China and Japan are currently in, so cool cultural sources must be modified. Apple-pie and Chevies give way to acupuncture and kimonos.

P O I N T   E I G H T

Try and take a completely opposite viewpoint to the mass It'll certainly get you noticed. but make sure you've done your homework. Taking the view that because of Volkswagens Hitler had quite a few redeeming qualities. or that the Ayatollah is OK because he likes Miles Davis, means you neglected to do your homework and deserve all the flack you get.

P O I N T   N I N E

You shouldn't have to read about cool in books So keep this one well hidden and only read it under the covers at night with your Durabeam torch.

P O I N T   S I X

Like everything, cool dates Velvet Underground. Vodka and lime. *Monty Python*. Psychedelia. Peace and love. Flares. Tolkien. Julie Ege posters. *Easy Rider*. *Magic Roundabout*. *Top of the Pops*. Sitting cross-legged. Studio 54. Muesli. Regines. Breakdancing. Singer-songwriters. Cowboy boots. Bullet Cartridge belts. Photographing Punks. Hampstead. **The solution.** Quit while you're ahead or do a 'David Bowie', [ie constantly change a successful formula by setting a new trend and staying one step ahead of the pack.]

P O I N T   T E N

There's always a need for cool people Especially nowadays with the world hotting up. Current statistics tell us that only one in 450 of the population are remotely cool. Unreleased government findings place the ratio as high as one in 603. . .

. . . it's up to you to bring down the odds.

COOL

COOL *Acknowledgements*

SPECIAL THANKS TO

John Walsh • Carolyn Hart •
Russell Ash • Peter Bridgewater •
Guy Holman • Laurie • Mike •
Marion • Paul • Peter • Carrie •
Matt the Brat • Julian Bajzert •
Camilla-June • Cathy Mellor •
Karen Ireland • Annie •
Sarah Coombe • Viv • Colin •
Terry • Lucian • Martin

C O O L

The publishers and the author would like to thank the following individuals, organisations, and agencies for supplying illustrations:

Alpha: pages 93, 125
Apple: page 69
Aston Martin Ltd: page 43
Bailey: page 131
Beserkley Records: page 71
British Aerospace: page 58
British Aircraft Corp: page 81
Camera Press: pages 12, 12, 15, 18, 19, 24, 25, 25, 60, 73, 120, 133
The Cinema Bookshop: page 99
Alan Davidson: page 62
EG Management/Brian Ferry: page 67
Ford Motor Co: page 54
Greenpeace: page 39
Billy Hamilton PR Ltd: page 57
Ilford Ltd: page 130
Jaguar Cars Ltd: page 55
Jarndyce Antiquarian Booksellers: page 116
Tahara Keiichi: page 89
The Kobal Collection: pages 8/9, 10, 10, 11, 11, 13, 14, 20/21, 22, 23, 27, 29, 29, 30, 31, 32, 33, 41, 45, 47, 49, 53, 56, 59, 61, 61, 63, 65, 66, 76, 77, 78, 79, 83, 85, 86, 90, 91, 97, 101, 102, 104/105, 106/107, 109, 110/111, 112, 123, 124, 129, 138
The London Electrotype Agency: pages 140/141
Lowe, Howard-Spink, Marschalk/Heineken: page 40

The Mansell Collection: page 98
David McGough/DMI: page 29
Michel & Co: page 35
Issey Miyake: page 88
The National Portrait Gallery: pages 26, 120
Network Photographers: pages 23, 74, 139
Marion Nitch-Smith: page 34
Pentax UK Ltd: page 98
Popperfoto: pages 16, 17, 19, 125, 128, 132
RCA Victor: page 71
Reliant: page 77
Rex Features: pages 38, 48
Rothschild: page 49
Ronald Searle: page 37
Seita – Gitanes: page 95
Standard Telephone: page 46
Steve: pages 59, 77, 94, 95, 113, 114, 115, 117, 121, 136/137
The Tate Gallery: page 127
Topham: page 44
Vertigo: page 7
Virgin Records Ltd: page 70
Volvo Concessionaires Ltd: page 13
Elizabeth Whiting Associates: page 43
Zippo: page 94

JACKET (Clockwise starting top left)
Rex Features, The Kobal Collection, The Kobal Collection, Camera Press, Popperfoto, Rex Features, Camera Press, The Kobal Collection, Popperfoto, Courtauld Institute of Art, Popperfoto, National Portrait Gallery